The Complete Guide To Securing Your Own U.S. Patent

A Step-By-Step Road Map To Protect Your Ideas and Inventions

With Companion CD-ROM

By
Jamaine Burrell

The Complete Guide to Securing Your Own U.S. Patent: A Step-By-Step Road Map To Protect Your Ideas and Inventions : With Companion CD-ROM

Copyright © 2007 Atlantic Publishing Group, Inc.
1405 SW 6th Avenue • Ocala, Florida 34474 • Phone 800-814-1132 • Fax 352-622-5836
Web site: www.atlantic-pub.com • E-mail: sales@atlantic-pub.com
SAN Number: 268-1250

ISBN-13: 978-0-910627-05-4 • ISBN-10: 0-910627-05-3

Library of Congress Cataloging-in-Publication Data
Burrell, Jamaine, 1958-
The complete guide to securing your own U.S. patent : A step-by-step road map to protect your ideas and inventions : with companion CD-ROM / by Jamaine Burrell.
    p. cm.
  Includes bibliographical references and index.
  ISBN-13: 978-0-910627-05-4 (alk. paper)
  ISBN-10: 0-910627-05-3 (alk. paper)
  1. Patent practice--United States--Popular works. 2. Patent laws and legislation--United States--Popular works. 3. Intellectual property--United States--Popular works. I. Title.

KF3120.Z9B868 2007
346.7304'86--dc22
                    2006034245

EDITOR: Marie Lujanac • mlujanac817@yahoo.com
FRONT COVER DESIGN & PROOFREADER: Angela C. Adams • angela.c.adams@hotmail.com
ART DIRECTION: Meg Buchner • megadesn@mchsi.com
PRODUCTION DESIGN: Sue Balcer: sue@justyourtype.biz
GLOSSARY COMPILED BY: Marie Lujanac • mlujanac817@yahoo.com

Printed on Recycled Paper

Printed in the United States

Chapter 7: Establishing Trade Secrets   95

Chapter 8: Establishing Patent Ownership   99

Chapter 9: The Patent Search   111

Chapter 10: Filing a Patent Application   129

Chapter 11: Parts of a Patent Application   147

We recently lost our beloved pet "Bear," who was not only our best and dearest friend but also the "Vice President of Sunshine" here at Atlantic Publishing. He did not receive a salary but worked tirelessly 24 hours a day to please his parents. Bear was a rescue dog that turned around and showered myself, my wife Sherri, his grandparents Jean, Bob and Nancy and every person and animal he met (maybe not rabbits) with friendship and love. He made a lot of people smile every day.

We wanted you to know that a portion of the profits of this book will be donated to The Humane Society of the United States.

–Douglas & Sherri Brown

THE HUMANE SOCIETY
OF THE UNITED STATES ©

The human-animal bond is as old as human history. We cherish our animal companions for their unconditional affection and acceptance. We feel a thrill when we glimpse wild creatures in their natural habitat or in our own backyard.

Unfortunately, the human-animal bond has at times been weakened. Humans have exploited some animal species to the point of extinction.

The Humane Society of the United States makes a difference in the lives of animals here at home and worldwide. The HSUS is dedicated to creating a world where our relationship with animals is guided by compassion. We seek a truly humane society in which animals are respected for their intrinsic value, and where the human-animal bond is strong.

Want to help animals? We have plenty of suggestions. Adopt a pet from a local shelter, join The Humane Society and be a part of our work to help companion animals and wildlife. You will be funding our educational, legislative, investigative and outreach projects in the U.S. and across the globe.

Or perhaps you'd like to make a memorial donation in honor of a pet, friend or relative? You can through our Kindred Spirits program. And if you'd like to contribute in a more structured way, our Planned Giving Office has suggestions about estate planning, annuities, and even gifts of stock that avoid capital gains taxes.

Maybe you have land that you would like to preserve as a lasting habitat for wildlife. Our Wildlife Land Trust can help you. Perhaps the land you want to share is a backyard—that's enough. Our Urban Wildlife Sanctuary Program will show you how to create a habitat for your wild neighbors.

So you see, it's easy to help animals. And The HSUS is here to help.

The Humane Society of the United States
2100 L Street NW
Washington, DC 20037
202-452-1100
www.hsus.org

Foreword

An invention, like a newborn baby, requires nurturing, understanding, and devotion from its inventor. No invention becomes a money-making product by simply patenting it. Someone has to bring the idea to "life" and make it accessible to as many users as possible; otherwise, it remains just a latent idea on a pile of papers.

This book takes the inventor through the arduous journey from the birth of the invention to the full-grown model to a salable product with a life all its own. Unlike other books that have been published in this area, this book provides clear direction in how to file your patent, maintain it, and develop it for use by the public so that you can earn royalties and income. The book gives precautionary measures, obscure deadlines, and possible pitfalls to avoid – all in clear straightforward, encouraging language.

I am a world-renowned inventor with more than 50 U.S. patents. My company, Anthony Engineering and Technologies, Inc., of Coral Springs, Florida, has developed many patents from concept to fully engineered, manufactured, and marketed products. Despite all my experience in patenting and developing products over the last 20 years, I have been able to provide my clients new information and resources by recommending this book and its guidelines. I am glad that this information has become available to the public. One of the most confusing aspects of inventing is gaining a clear understanding of the costs and work involved in bringing a product to life. Sometimes inventors know what the end result should be but do not know how to get there legally. This book provides a good road map for the serious inventor

To the new Edisons out there I say, read this book carefully and use it to your best advantage.

Michael M. Anthony
CEO, President,
Anthony Engineering and Technologies Inc.
10189 W. Sample Road,
Coral Springs, Florida 33065
www.anthonyeng.com

Introduction

T his book is an accumulation of documented research on inventions, IP rights, and IP assets as they relate to U.S. patents. Though foreign patents are discussed, this book is not intended to provide details about acquiring patents outside the United States. Nor is it intended to provide details about acquiring U.S. patents by parties outside of the United States. Unless otherwise specified, all references to patents are intended to mean U.S. patents.

This book addresses U.S. patent law as it was understood at the time of writing. It will not attempt to rationalize, justify, or quantify any decision or request made by the U.S. Patent and Trademark Office (PTO), or any other patent office, with respect to patenting an invention or declining a patent for an invention. The patentability of any one invention is established and defined on its own merits, as determined by the PTO. Laws regarding patents and patent rights change periodically, particularly as they relate to music and licensing music patents.

Patents, whether being sought in the U.S. or elsewhere, must be properly applied for with documentation and drawings, if applicable, of the various views of the invention to be patented.

This book does not detail the specifics of the graphic design necessary to create such drawings. However, it does characterize the basic elements of patent drawings.

Though the primary subject of this book is a U.S. patent, Chapters five, six, and seven are devoted to the other IP assets, namely copyrights, trademarks, and trade secrets, respectively. The remaining chapters are then entirely devoted to patents.

Chapter One, *What Is a U.S. Patent?*, attempts to define patents, types of patents, rights offered by various types of patents, the patent filing process, and patent requirements for an invention to fit into a statutory class.

Chapter Two, *Inventions*, discusses processes necessary to design and develop an invention for patentability, the objectives of inventing, the importance of documentation during the design and development phase, methods of documenting an invention, invention prototypes, and the prototyping process.

Chapter Three, *Intellectual Property (IP)*, discusses intellectual property, rights, assets, copyright, trademark, trade secret, and patent laws.

Chapter Four, *Contractual IP Rights*, discusses contracts, royalties, types of licenses, licensing as it applies to patents.

Chapter Five, *Establishing Copyrights*, discusses establishing and maintaining copyright protection for original works of authorship (OWAs), copyright limitations, registering, licensing, and using a copyright.

Chapter Six, *Establishing Trademarks*, discusses establishing and maintaining the commercial identifier known as a trademark and registering and using a trademark.

Chapter Seven, *Establishing Trade Secrets*, discusses establishing and maintaining trade secrets as well as trade secret policies.

Chapter Eight, *Establishing Patent Ownership*, discusses patent ownership issues involving the inventor/owner, the employer/owner, and forms of joint ownership.

Chapter Nine, *The Patent Search*, discusses the need for and methods of a patent search, searching PTO resources, PTDLs, professional patent searchers, the search process, search limitations, and search results.

Chapter Ten, *Filing a Patent Application*, discusses types of patent applications, the processes necessary to make application for a patent in the U.S. and abroad as well as the necessary documentation that must accompany an application. It also includes a discussion of the benefit of member treaties with the U.S.

Chapter Eleven, *"Parts of a Patent Application"*, provides a discussion of the patent application, individual parts of a patent application and supporting documents that must accompany an application.

Chapter Twelve, *"Patent Application Processing"*, provides a discussion of the processes and methods used by the PTO in examining, evaluating and issuing a patent. It includes a discussion of office actions as well as application rejections, objections, amendments and corrections.

Chapter Thirteen, *Marketing and Manufacturing a Patented Invention*, provides a discussion of methods to promote, manufacture, distribute, and sell a patented invention - even using an intermediary to assist in the process.

Chapter Fourteen, *Protecting a Patent*, discusses patent protection, particularly infringement, methods to stop infringement, and defenses against infringement.

Biz Wiz Says...

Throughout the chapters you'll find boxes such as this one highlighting a particularly important tip or thought from Mathew J. Temmerman, a registered patent attorney with backgrounds in Biology and Electrical Engineering, practicing out of Davis, California. He may be contacted at the Temmerman Law Office at 530-750-3661.

Mathew's tips and stories serve as extra reminders to do the obvious, even when it isn't.

chapter one

What is a U.S. Patent?

A U.S. patent is a legal right granted by the U.S. government to protect an invention. The U.S. Patent and Trademark Office (PTO), a division of the U. S. Department of Commerce, is the government organization responsible for issuing patents and performing related duties. A patent grants an inventor the right to exclude another party from selling, making, using, or offering the invention for sale in the United States or importing the invention into the United States for a fixed time period. Under certain circumstances, patent rights are also extended to heirs and assignees of the inventor. In general, a patent has a life span of 14 to 20 years from the date of filing application for it in the U.S., so long as required maintenance fees are paid to secure and maintain the patent.

In the U.S., an inventor may file two types of patent applications: a provisional application is a relatively new form of a patent application that was established to provide inventors with a method of documenting the development of an invention and establishing an early priority date without the expense associated with a non-provisional patent application. A non-provisional patent application is the traditional and official application that the PTO processes and examines. A provisional patent application must be followed, within one-year, by the filing of a non-provisional patent application, or else the PTO destroys the provisional application. As such, the granting of a patent is determined by information provided in the non-provisional application. Since a provisional application serves as a sort of temporary application that expires after one year, reference to patent applications are intended to mean non-provisional applications, unless otherwise specified.

If a patent application contains specific reference to a previously filed patent application, the date of filing is established as the date of the previously filed application, provided assessed maintenance fees were paid for the previously filed application. Upon expiration, it cannot be renewed. However, under certain special circumstances, the life of patents may be extended beyond 20 years.

Patent rights extend throughout the 50 states and all U.S. possessions and territories, but those rights to not apply to patents acquired outside of the U.S. borders. International treaties provide reciprocal filing rules and the right of priority for U.S. patent owners who want to acquire patent rights in other countries. So long as established procedures are followed, reciprocal filing rules provide that a U.S. patent owner be treated in the same manner as citizens in the particular foreign nation where patents rights are being sought. The right of priority provides for a U.S. patent owner to file for patent protection in all member countries of the treaty within a specified time and be given the same filing date as that used for the U.S. patent. The protection provided by a patent begins on the date on which an invention is disclosed. When an inventor creates a written invention disclosure, the inventor establishes a "date of original conception." U.S. patents are issued on a first-to-invent basis. The first party to establish a date of original conception is the party entitled to a valid patent for the disclosed invention.

Although the United States still uses a first-to-invent system, inventors should not delay in filing a patent application. Courts have unsympathetically invalidated patents due to delays in filing even where the delay was only due to lack of finances!

Types of U.S. Patents

U. S. Patents are issued as one of three types, which include utility patents, design patents, and plant patents. Of the three types of patents, utility patents are the most commonly issued. They protect inventions that uniquely serve to produce a utilitarian result, which means the invention must be useful and functional. Design patterns differ from utility patents. Design patents protect the design pattern of an object. The protected design must have no effect on the functionality of the object to which it is associated. Plant patents differ from utility and design patents because plant patents protect pollination, which is the invention of sexually reproducible plants. Under special circumstances, utility patents have also been used to protect sexually reproducible plants, but in general, utility patents are used to protect asexually reproducible plants.

The time from the date of filing application for a patent to the date of issuance is known as the patent pendency period. No patent rights may be exercised during the pendency period, unless the application is published. If patent rights are violated during the pendency period of a published patent application, the applicant may seek royalties for the infringement. Further, when the patent is issued, the patent will serve the purpose of preventing any further infringement.

Utility Patents

Utility patents protect inventions that are useful, meaning they offer utility. The utility offered by an invention must be functional, not aesthetic, and the inventor must be capable of proving that the invention actually serves a useful purpose. Virtually any type of invention may be claimed to provide some form of utility, but patent laws define some inventions as useless. Inventions that are frivolous, illegal, immoral, inoperable, or aesthetic as well as inventions that are composed of unsafe drugs, nuclear weaponry, or theoretical phenomena are considered to be useless. Utility patents, issued as a result of application made before June 7, 1995, expire 17 years after their issuance. Changes in patent laws in 1995 extended the time to 20 years. The expiration period for certain utility patents may be further extended to compensate for delays in the patent examination process. The expiration period may be extended if any of the following situations arise:

- The PTO fails to complete examination of a new patent application within 14 months of filing such application.

- The PTO fails to issue a patent within three years from the filing of the application. The PTO, not the inventor, must be responsible for causing or instigating the delay.

- The PTO fails to act for more than four months for certain office actions.

- Commercial marketing is delayed because of regulatory review, such as those required by the Environmental Protection Agency (EPA) or the Food and Drug Administration (FDA).

Patent laws dictate that patents protecting certain drugs may have the term of expiration extended up to five years to compensate for delays in marketing due to federal pre-marketing regulatory procedures.

Design Patents

Design patents protect the visible uniqueness in the design or shape of an object. Design patents only protect the appearance of an object, not its functionality. A pair of jeans, for example, functions as clothing. Once a unique design is stitched on the pocket, the jeans may be patented under a design patent because of the uniqueness of the design, not because the stitching serves any utilitarian purpose. If the pant legs of the jeans were equipped with a zipper at knee length such that the jeans could be converted to shorts, the jeans would then serve a utilitarian purpose. The dual use jeans would then be patentable under a utility patent, not a design patent. Unlike utility patents, design patents expire 14 years after the date of issuance.

The three legal requirements for a design patent include the following:

1. **The design must be new and original, thus novel.** Novelty implies that the design must differ from all designs used in prior art. The design must also be original, meaning the design cannot imitate any existing design. A design that depicts a naturally occurring object may or may not be considered original, dependent upon how it is displayed. In general, a patentable design must result from industry, effort, genius, or expense. When a design simulates an existing and well-known object it is not considered original.

2. **The design must be non-obvious.** When a new design is obvious to others in the particular field of the design, the design does not meet the requirements to be patented. A design is novel if it does not exist as prior art. However, most designs evolve from existing designs. A designer may create non-obviousness by using a familiar art form in an unfamiliar medium, making a slight change to an existing

design, omitting a visual component of an existing design or rearranging elements of an existing design to create an unexpected visual result. If a design is created in such a fashion and also meets certain other criteria, as listed below, the design is more likely to meet the requirement of non-obviousness and patentability is most probable. Patentability is more likely if the design:

- Has enjoyed commercial success.

- Has an unexpected visual appearance.

- Has been copied by others.

- Has been praised by others in the field.

- Has been tried, but was not successful or is created despite the contention that it could not be done.

A design is non-obvious if no one has already considered making the design. A design that is non-obvious to others in the particular field of the design is patentable.

3. **The design must be an ornamental design for a useful article of manufacture.** The ornamental design of an object includes three common components: proportion, surface ornamentation, or the combination of shape and ornamentation. A design must be a definite, preconceived article that is capable of being reproduced. It must be static. It may not be dynamically produced, such as with randomly generated patterns, even if the same series of patterns is reproducible. A design must be primarily ornamental and not dictated by an article's function. The design must be visible during the normal intended use or during commercial use. Designs that are intermittently hidden, such as with the insoles of shoes, may be patented so long as the design is embodied on an article of manufacture.

Plant Patents

Plant patents protect plants that are asexually reproduced, primarily by grafting and cutting. Patents issued to protect plants may be issued as either plant patents or utility patents. Plant patents are issued for the asexual reproduction of plants, which includes any type of reproduction that does not rely upon the use of seeds. Asexual reproduction is usually accomplished by grafting or cloning plant tissue. In addition to incorporating an asexual method of reproduction, a plant patent must also be novel and distinctive. Plant patents may not be issued for plants that exist in an uncultivated state or plants that are tuber-propagated.

Utility patents may be issued for both sexual and asexual plants or elements of such plants. Elements of plants may include genes, protein, pollen, fruit, DNA, buds, or chemicals extracted from plants as well as the methods used in the manufacture of plants. Utility patents are issued for man-made plants so long as the plant meets the requirements for utility, novelty, and non-obviousness. A plant patent must include claims that describe specific characteristics of the plant. An inventor may justify such claims by depositing seeds or plant tissue from the plant at a public depository. The United States and many other countries have established International Depository Authorities to suit such a purpose.

A plant patent is more easily acquired for a plant than a utility patent, but a utility patent provides a broader scope of protection for plants. Infringing upon a plant patent can only be accomplished if the actual patented plant is asexually reproduced. The infringing plant must have the same genetics as the patented plant, not just the same general characteristics. On the other hand, infringement upon a utility patent for a plant may occur with either sexual or asexual reproduction of the plant. It should be noted that the protection provided by a utility patent for a plant prevents another party from making, manufacturing, or using the seed line; it does not prevent another party from selling the resulting plant.

Plant patents issued as a result of application made before June 7, 1995, expire 17 years after their issuance. Changes in patent laws extend the time from 17 years to 20 years for patents that were applied for after that date.

Biz Wiz Says . . . "In general, a U.S. patent only provides protection in the United States. For instance, if a knock-off product is being produced in China and sold in a country other than the U.S., a U.S. patent would be powerless to stop it."

Offensive Rights vs. Protection

The language of patents always includes the term protection, but one must understand that patents only provide offensive protection, not defensive protection. In other words, patent rights are exercised in offense of a violator's action to infringe on the patent. Patents will not prevent another party from selling, making, importing, using, or offering a patented invention for sale. Anyone may make, use, offer for sale, sell, or import the invention without issuance of a grant to do so from the government. The patent holder must be responsible to exercise the IP rights provided by a patent and sue the party in violation of those rights.

Patents give an inventor or invention owner the "right to exclude" others from infringing on an invention. A patent does not grant the inventor or invention owner the right to make, use, offer for sale, sell, or import his or her own invention, if such patent rights infringe on the existing patent rights of another patent owner, violate the rights of other individuals or violate any laws. A patent grants only the exclusive nature of the right. A patent, for example, may not be used to violate federal anti-trust laws.

Requirements for a Patent

The PTO is responsible to preserve, classify, and disseminate patent information in an effort to encourage innovation and to advance science and technology. As the name implies, the PTO issues patents to protect inventions, and they also register trademarks to protect business service identifications and corporate products. One must file an application with this organization to receive a patent. A PTO examiner inspects the submitted materials and makes a decision as to the sufficiency of the invention to meet patent law requirements. More than one-half of all submitted applications fail to have a patent issued because the applicants fail to meet one of the four basic requirements for patentability. The invention must fit into a statutory class and it must also meet the requirements for usefulness, novelty, and non-obviousness. If application is made for a utility patent, the application must also meet certain legal requirements.

The requirements for a patent make no consideration for the personal status of the applicant. No consideration may be made for the following personal attributes:

• Sex	• Age	• Creed	• Race
• Mental Competence	• Country of Residence	• Citizenship	• Natural Origin
• Health	• Physical Disability	• Nationality	• Religion
• Incarceration			

A patent may be issued to an adult or a child. A patent may also be issued through a personal representative for a deceased or mentally challenged person. A patent may be issued to U.S. citizens as well as citizens of foreign nations.

To sustain a patent and keep it in force, maintenance fees must be paid for the patent. A complete schedule of fees, including maintenance fees, which are charged by the PTO, is included at Appendix I (US PTO Fee Schedule). Fees are required to be paid 3½, 7½, and 11½ years after the original patent is issued from applications filed on and after December 12, 1980. Maintenance fees must be paid at the specified time intervals, and they do not require a surcharge if payment is made within the six-month window of opportunity preceding the due date. Otherwise, a surcharge is applied to the late payment of fees. The PTO will not send notice of the maintenance fee due unless payment is not made on time. In such a case, the PTO will issue the responsible party of record a notice informing the recipient of the consequence of making payment during the grace period. Payment made during the grace period incurs no surcharge.

Statutory Classes

The U.S. Congress has established five statutory classes of patents. A patented invention must meet the requirements of at least one of these classes. Statutory classes do not apply to natural phenomena, the laws of nature, or abstractions. An invention may fall into more than one statutory class. The PTO, not the inventor, determines the final classification of an invention. The five statutory classes include the following:

1. **Processes.** Processes, also called methods, include ways of doing or making things that involve more than mental intellect. Processes may include one or more steps to express an activity or manipulate a physical object. Processes may

include purely manual processes and software.

Traditional processes have included various types of chemical reactions and treatments, which are responsible to change the composition of an object or change the method of creating products and chemicals. Modern day processes also include computer software or programs. Rules regarding the patenting of software are still evolving, but in general, software may be patented as either a process or a machine (discussed below under "Machines"). To be classified as a process, software must have some effect on a piece of hardware or another process. The software must produce some concrete, useful, and tangible result. The requirement that software affect a piece of hardware predates the requirement for software to affect another process. Some critics of the PTO question whether the PTO can adequately assess the more technically challenging requirement of the software's effect on other software or the existence of prior art in this field of information technology.

2. **Machines.** Machines include devices or other objects used to accomplish a task. Machines involve activity or motion as performed by working parts. Unlike with processes, the focus is on the working parts rather than methods that ensure that the parts work. Processes create work while machines do work. Software may be patented as a machine when a patent claim includes language that indicates the software provides a means to perform some type of activity.

3. **Articles of Manufacture.** Articles of manufacture include simple objects made by either humans or machines. In general, the primary feature of articles of manufacture is that they have few or no working parts. Machines that are simplistic or have few working parts may also be categorized as articles of manufacture.

4. **Compositions of Matter.** Compositions of matter include matter that is composed of chemically significant substances. Compositions may be supplied in solid, liquid, or gaseous forms. Naturally occurring matter cannot be patented as a composition of matter unless it is patented as a purified form of such matter. Some compositions may also be classified as articles of manufacture; however, compositions of matter are more concerned with chemical compositions than the physical shapes or forms of matter.

5. **New use of any of the above.** A "new use" of an existing invention is the discovery of a new use for the invention as opposed to the invention of a new process or object. A new use must offer novelty and non-obviousness. As such, the new use of an invention is, technically, a process that is specifically categorized as a new use.

Usefulness

The requirement for usefulness requires that an invention serve some useful purpose or utility. Any form of usefulness or utility that also offers functionality and is not aesthetic may be patentable. A patent application must clearly state a realistic use. The PTO deems the following types of inventions useless and will not issue patents for their use.

- **Unsafe Drugs.** Patent applications for new drugs or new uses of existent drugs must indicate an ability of the drug to treat some verifiable condition. In addition, the drug must be proven safe for the intended purpose. The PTO recognizes certain drugs as safe and characterizes them in a safe chemical category. The Food and Drug Administration (FDA) must approve all other drugs for use before the PTO will consider issuing a patent for them.

- **Whimsical Inventions.** Some inventions, though documented to serve a useful purpose, have uses that are considered to be whimsical. In 1937, under patent No. 2,079,053, the PTO patented a windshield for a horse with a tail-operated windshield wiper. The utility of the invention was documented as amusement. This type of whimsical invention would be rejected in modern day patenting processes.

- **Inventions that Serve an Illegal Purpose.** In general, the PTO will not issue patents for inventions that are intended to serve an illegal purpose. However, the language of patent claims may be manipulated to allow for the establishment of such patents. An invention that is capable of copying currency, for example, may be patented if the language of the claims indicates that the invention will be used to test the ability to copy currency rather than to actually copy the currency.

- **Inventions that are Deemed Immoral.** In general, the PTO will not issue patents for inventions that are considered immoral. However, the definition of immoral continues to be debated. In past years, for example, the PTO has refused to issue patents for sexual stimulants and sex toys because of issues of morality. In modern day, these types of inventions are no longer considered immoral and are patentable.

- **Inventions that are Inoperable.** The PTO requires that an invention be operable and that the patent application clearly indicate how to make the invention work. The burden of proving that an invention is operable falls on the patent applicant. The PTO includes examiners with technically oriented backgrounds who will perform very stringent analytical testing to ensure that an invention works as described

- **Nuclear Weaponry.** Special statute, resulting from the U.S. Atomic Energy Act, dictates that nuclear materials and atomic energy, when utilized as components of weaponry, are not patentable.

- **Theories.** Theoretical phenomena, laws of nature, and abstractions are not patentable.

- **Patents that Serve Only an Aesthetic Purpose.** Inventions that serve only aesthetic functions have no utility as a design patent or utility patent and are not patentable.

Novelty

The requirement for novelty is that the invention be different from any other known to the public. If a new invention presents any difference, no matter how small, from an existing invention, the new invention meets the requirement for novelty. A new invention may be composed of new physical features, a new combination of old features, or a new use of old features.

Prior Art

The requirement for novelty is that an invention be physically different from any previous invention, which implies that the invention cannot replicate what is known. What is already known is considered prior art. Patent laws specifically define prior art as the state of knowledge existing or publicly available either before the date of the invention or more than one year prior to the patent application date. The latter is referred to as the "one-year rule." The one-year rule applies to the application for either a provisional patent or a non-provisional patent.

One-Year Rule

Patent laws dictate that an inventor must file a U.S. patent application within one year of the following acts:

- Offering the invention for sale

- Selling the invention

- Commercially using or describing the invention

- Publicly using or describing the invention

If the inventor fails to file for patent under the one-year rule, the inventor is barred from obtaining a patent. If the PTO issues a patent for an invention, but the inventor failed to abide by the one-year rule and the PTO later finds that the inventor violated the rule, the issued patent may be declared invalid.

The one-year rule applies only to U.S. patents. It is not applicable if the inventor intends to file for a foreign patent. Most foreign governments require that a patent not be offered for sale, sold, publicly used, or published before filing for a U.S. patent. However, international patent agreements, shared by major industrialized counties, allow an inventor to offer the invention for sale, sell the invention, or publish the invention without losing foreign patent rights so long as the inventor files for the foreign patent within one year of filing in the United States. In countries that are not party to such an international patent treaty, the inventor is required to file for a U.S. patent before publicizing the invention to meet their requirements for a patent.

Date of Invention

The date of invention is defined as the earliest of the following three dates:

1. **The date the inventor filed for a patent application**. Each patent application has a date of filing that is documented on the application.

2. **The date of reduction to practice.** The date of reduction to practice is the date on which the invention was built and tested in either the United States, a signatory nation of the North American Free Trade Association (NAFTA),

or a signatory nation of World Trade Organization (WTO). Most industrialized nations are members of the WTO. A reduction to practice exists when an inventor is capable of demonstrating that the invention works as intended. There are two methods an inventor may use to demonstrate a reduction to practice. They include an actual reduction to practice and a constructive reduction to practice. An actual reduction to practice involves building and testing the invention as well as demonstrating that the invention works as intended. A constructive reduction to practice

Bíz Wíz Says ... Many inventors come to me believing they must either submit or have available an actual working prototype of the invention, but for U.S. law this is not the case. Constructive reduction to practice is enough.

involves preparing a patent application that demonstrates how to make the invention, how to use the invention, and how the invention works.

3. **The date the invention was conceived in a NAFTA or WTO country.** The date an invention was conceived in a NAFTA or WTO nation is determined from documentation that describes the invention and that inventors are required to maintain while designing, developing, building, and testing the invention. This type of documentation is important because it serves as the only proof of the date of conception, should it come into question. A date of conception must be supplemented with documented proof of reduction to practice (building and testing the invention) or the date of conception will be as determined

by the filing date of a patent application for the invention. Documentation for an invention is essential in determining and justifying dates of reduction to practice and dates of conception. These dates are usually established months before a non-provisional patent application is filed, and they become significant when determining the existence of prior art.

Printed Publications

Prior art includes any printed publication, printed anywhere in the world, in any language, by any author, which is published anytime before the date of invention or more than one year before an inventor makes application for a patent. Printed publications include patents, books, magazines, journals, technical papers, abstracts, or any photocopy of such items. Printed publications also include information that is publicly accessible on the Internet. Patents are the most referenced forms of prior art used by the PTO. If a patent is pending for an invention, but not yet issued, the pending patent is considered prior art for any patent application filed or any date of invention established during the pendency period.

Prior Public Knowledge or Prior Use

Prior art need not be in the form of a written document. Any form of public knowledge or public use may constitute prior art. If at least one person is allowed to make use of an invention without restriction, the use of the invention may be considered as prior art. If the inventor fails to file application for a patent as specified by the one-year rule, the inventor forfeits any rights to protect the invention against infringement as provided by patent laws. An otherwise infringing party is free to make use of the invention. If, however, the invention was publicly known or publicly used for experimental purposes, the one-year rule for making application for a patent does not take effect until the experimentation is complete. The use of an invention does not qualify as prior use during the experimental stage.

Prior art includes an invention that was first applied for patent in a foreign nation. If a U.S. patent application is filed more than one year after making application for the patent in a foreign nation or after the foreign patent is issued, the issued or pending patent represents prior art for the invention.

Prior Sale or On-Sale Status

When an invention is not publicized in written form but is offered for sale, sold, or used commercially, the inventor must make application for a patent within one year after the offer, sale, or commercial use as part of the one-year rule The one-year rule applies to the commercial offer or sale of a hardware invention or a process that embodies the invention even if the invention is not yet completed. The invention, however, must be drawn or described in reasonable detail such that it is not interpreted to represent a concept, but a piece of hardware or a process. If a sale is made to test the commercial feasibility of the invention, the inventor risks violating patent rights in foreign nations. Most foreign governments insist that an invention not be offered for sale, sold, publicly used, or published before filing a patent application for the invention in the United States.

Patent Interference

If two parties file an application to patent the same or substantially the same invention, the PTO declares interference between the two parties. Interference is resolved by proceedings to establish the first inventor to reduce the invention to a practice or the first inventor to conceive the invention and then reduce it to a practice. Conception refers to completion, with respect to devising a means for accomplishing a result. Conception is the process of developing or creating an invention. Reduction to practice refers to the physical construction of an invention. Physical construction of a machine involves actually building the machine. Physical construction of an article of manufacture or composition of matter is the making of the article or matter. The physical construction of a process involves carrying out the steps of the process. An actual demonstration, operation, or test of the intended use may also be required to prove construction. The filing of a non-provisional patent application that completely discloses an invention is usually equated to a reduction to practice.

About 1 percent of all patent applications filed in the U.S. require an interference proceeding. Interference may also occur between a patent application and a patent that has already been issued. The issued patent must have been issued within one year of the filing of the conflicting application. The conflicting application must actually be patentable and not barred from patentability for some other reason.

Each party to an interference proceeding must be capable of presenting evidence of the fact that the invention was made. Evidence includes various facts and circumstances pertaining to the development of the invention. If a party is not capable of presenting such evidence, the filing date of the patent application is determined by the earliest date of conception. Three administrative patent judges from the PTO's Board of Patent Appeals and Interference examine the evidence and determine priority based on conception or reduction to practice. The losing party may appeal the decision to the Court of Appeals for the Federal Circuit or file a civil action against the winning party in an appropriate U.S. district court.

Abandonment

An abandoned patent is a patent for which an invention is

published or used, but no patent application is filed. If the PTO becomes aware that an issued patent had been abandoned, the patent will be ruled invalid. Abandonment does not include a work stoppage or inaction due to health issues, financial issues, or the lack of a crucial part of an invention. Patent laws allow for the PTO to excuse inaction in the patenting process under such circumstances. The burden of proof, however, falls on the inventor to prove that inaction is legitimate and not abandonment.

Physical Differences

The requirement for novelty is that an invention be different, meaning it must present some type of physical or structural differences over prior art. Differences must exist in contrast to the most similar prior art and those differences must be non-obvious to an individual with ordinary skills in the particular area of technology that relates to the invention. Physical differences in a hardware invention may include such things as a non-obvious difference in shape, size, composition, or color from what is already known. Physical differences do not include such characteristics as faster, lighter, or safer. These characteristics represent different results or advantages, not physical differences. Physical differences in a process invention require that the new process modify a critical area of a prior art. As such, a new invention may be composed entirely of prior art if the new invention includes a new combination of old components used in prior art.

Non-Obviousness

The requirement for non-obviousness is that the invention be innovative and not obvious to others skilled in the particular art at the time the invention was created. Non-obviousness is demonstrated with new inventions that present knowledge or features that are superior, unexpected, or surprising. The fact that inventions are thought to be obvious is the main reason for PTO objections. Non-obviousness is the most misunderstood requirement for obtaining a patent.

Non-obviousness and the production of new and different results are often confused with novel physical differences. The PTO considers a new invention that produces new results to be an issue of non-obviousness. If the new results are surprising or unexpected, the invention is considered non-obvious. The requirement for novelty is that an invention have physical differences from what is already known. Physical differences do not necessarily constitute surprising or unexpected results, though it is possible for such differences to have those characteristics.

Ordinary Skill

Non-obviousness requires that the invention be non-obvious to a person having ordinary skill in the field of art represented by the invention at the time of its creation. A person who has ordinary skills in a particular field is one who works in the field and is, hypothetically, knowledgeable of all prior art in the field. Hypothetic knowledge stems from the understanding that no one person can be knowledgeable of all potential inventions that may be developed in one field of art. The PTO considers one that is reasonably knowledgeable of the underlying subject matter pertaining to an invention to be sufficiently knowledgeable to act as an expert in the particular field of art and thus, has hypothetical knowledge in the field of the invention.

Secondary Factors

The Supreme Court has the final say as to the non-obviousness of an invention. As such, the Supreme Court has established a five-step approach to determining non-obviousness as follows:

1. Determine the scope and content of all accessible prior art.

2. Determine the novelty of the invention.

3. Determine the level of skill required for artisans in the field of art.

4. Against the background of these artists, determine the obviousness or non-obviousness of the invention.

5. Consider secondary and objective factors that influence the determination of obviousness. Specifically, determine whether the invention has enjoyed commercial success, whether it fulfills a long felt but unresolved need, and whether others have failed to come up with the invention.

Other secondary factors that may be taken into consideration by the courts or PTO in the establishment of non-obviousness include the following:

- The invention solves a problem that had never been recognized by prior art.

- The invention solves a problem that is documented in prior art as insoluble.

- The invention demonstrates an advance in a field of art that is mature and already has many successful patents.

- The invention functions with the omission of a part or element that was necessary in prior art, particularly if the omission is responsible to reduce the expense, reliability, or labor required for the invention.

- The invention modifies prior art in a manner that had never been suggested before.

- The invention introduces an advantage that had not been appreciated in prior art.

- The invention solves an operational problem that was not included in prior art.

- The invention is a successful implementation of an ancient idea.

- The invention is capable of functioning or operating contrary to prior art teachings that indicate an impossibility.

- The invention consists of more than one element of prior art, the combination of which must produce new or unexpected results.

Secondary factors that may be taken into consideration by the PTO in establishing non-obviousness for combination inventions include the following:

- The invention is synergistic, such that the results achieved by the combination invention are greater than the results achieved by the individual components documented in prior art.

- The invention is composed of components that were never suggested or implied in prior art references.

- The invention is composed of a combination of prior art references indicated or implied to be an impossible combination.

- The invention is combined differently from prior art combinations of the same elements, particularly when the new combination reduces the complexity of the combination.

- The invention functions or operates contrary to prior art references that indicate the combination could not be operational.

- The invention includes elements that are similar to those referred to in prior art of a different field of interest.

Filing a Patent Application

When an inventor or invention owner makes application for a patent with the PTO, the PTO is responsible to process the patent application and determine if the applicant is entitled to a patent based upon established patent laws. The PTO performs a number of duties with respect to applied patents, which include the following:

- Examining patent applications.

- Issuing patents for inventions when the applicant has met the established requirements for a patent.

- Publishing issued patents.

- Publishing patent information.

- Recording patent assignments.

- Maintaining search files of U.S. and foreign patents.

- Providing public assess to search files.

- Making patents and related official records available to the public.

Though the PTO performs a number of patent related duties, it has no jurisdiction over infringement, enforcement, promotion, or the use of patents or inventions. The PTO also performs similar duties with respect to the registering of trademarks.

Upon acceptance of a patent application, the party making application for the patent is required to pay a filing fee before a patent is actually issued. The PTO Fee Schedule as last revised in May 2006 is included at Appendix I. Patent application filing fees are subject to change each October. Applicants must be sure to verify the required fees before making submission and payment to the PTO. The filing fee for non-provisional, utility patent applications includes a basic fee that entitles the applicant to

Bíz Wíz Says . . . In actuality, the length of time from submission to examination varies greatly depending on the technology field of the subject matter of the patent. For certain art fields, the length of time to initial examination can be as long as three years. For simple mechanical inventions, the length of time to initial examination can be very short, even under one year.

include 20 claims with no more than three in independent form. An additional fee is required for each additional claim in excess of the 20 allowed and for each additional claim in independent form that is in excess of the three allowed for the basic fee. An additional fee is also required if the application includes multiple dependent claims. A single claim is in dependent form if it refers to and incorporates a single preceding claim. The preceding claim may be either dependent or independent. A multiple claim is considered to be in dependent form in accordance with the number of claims to which reference is made. Additional fees may also be assessed if additional claims are presented after the application is filed, such as with an amended application. If the applicant is a small investor, small business or non-profit organization, filing fees are reduced by one-half, provided the applicant includes documentation that verifies the applicant's status as a small entity.

Processing a Patent Application

Processing a patent application by the PTO is a lengthy process. Processing and examination of a patent application takes about two years. After a rigorous examination of submitted materials, the PTO makes a decision as to the issuance of the patent. The PTO publishes a Manual of Patent Examining Procedures (MPEP) that outlines the Rules of Practice governing issuance of patents.

Patent examiners are grouped according to their expertise in a particular patentable field of technology. After the PTO receives a patent application, an appropriately skilled patent examiner performs a patent search of all patents that appear relevant to the invention, as it is defined in the application. The patent examiner then examines all relevant and existing prior art references as provided with the application to determine whether any novel physical differences exist with the new invention. If the new invention presents new physical features, new combinations, or new uses of prior art as defined by the requirement for patent novelty, the examiner must then determine if the novelty produces any unexpected or surprising results as defined by the requirement for patent non-obviousness. If the patent examiner is not capable of easily identifying the non-obviousness of the invention, the application is rejected. This type of rejection is common in the initial stages of the patent process and is termed a "shotgun "or "shoot-from-the-hip" rejection. A shotgun rejection simply informs the inventor that he or she is responsible to explain to the patent examiner how the invention meets the requirement for

Bíz Wíz Says . . . Only one original copy of the patent will ever be issued, even if it is lost or destroyed. While losing the original patent does not affect one's legal rights, the original should nevertheless be kept in a safe place.

non-obviousness. If the inventor is successful, a reexamination of the patent application takes place. If the inventor is not successful in convincing the patent examiner of non-obviousness, the issue may be settled in court.

Court action requires the expertise of a patent attorney or other experts familiar with the technical aspects of the invention. Both the inventor and the PTO will be expected to acquire services of professionals to argue their particular case for or against non-obviousness. The objective is to prove that the invention does or does not produce new and unexpected results as required for non-obviousness.

Patent Allowance

On examination of a patent application or at a later time during a reconsideration of a patent application, the application may be found to be allowable. A notice of allowance is sent to the applicant or the applicant's attorney or agent of record. Upon receipt of a notice of allowance, the applicant is required to pay a fee for the issuance of the patent. The fee is due within three months of the notice. If payment is not received within the three-month time, the patent application will be considered abandoned. Statutes allow for a late payment of the required fee when a delay in payment is proven to be unavoidable. A patent is issued as soon as possible after the date of payment of the fee, but the actual grant of the patent is dependent upon the volume of printing required for the paper copy of the patent. A patent grant is delivered or mailed on the day on which the grant is issued or as soon as possible thereafter. The grant is delivered to the applicant or the applicant's agent or attorney of record. Also, on the date of the grant, the patent file becomes open to the public and printed copies of the associated specification and drawings become publicly available. If publication of an invention is considered to be detrimental to the national defense, patent laws give the PTO the power to withhold the grant of the patent, and to order the invention secret for such time period as required by national interests.

Patents are issued in the name of the United States and under the seal of the PTO. Either the "Commissioner of Patents and Trademarks" is included as the signatory or an official of the PTO attests the Commissioner's written signature. When a patent is issued to an applicant, the applicant receives a grant of the application, annexed by a printed copy of the specification and drawings. The grant indicates "the right to exclude others from making, using, offering for sale, or selling the invention throughout the United States or importing the invention into the United States." Reference to the United States implies the U.S. and each of its territories and possessions.

Any instrument related to a patent should be identified with the patent number, date, name of the inventor, and title of the invention as specified in the patent. Any instrument related to a patent application should identify the application number, date of filing, name of the inventor, and title of the invention as specified in the application. If a patent application is assigned and executed at the same time that an application is being prepared but before it is filed with the PTO, the assignment should identify the application by its date of execution, name of the inventor, and title of the invention so that no mistakes are made as to the identity of the applicant.

chapter two

Inventions

For centuries, inventions have plotted the future of our country. They have stimulated prosperity and commerce and transformed the country into the powerhouse of industry, manufacturing, and technology that we enjoy today. Cars, personal computers, cell phones, the Internet, and television are just a few of the inventions that were created just in the past century, and inventors have made fortunes from them. An invention may be a device, machine, life form, process, or method, or it may be a new use of an existing invention. An invention is generally defined to be any new machine, article, process, development, or use. The United States leads the world in inventions and innovation, but many inventions have never made it to market. To develop an invention is one thing. To bring it to market for sale is quite another. What many inventors lack is the knowledge to develop their ideas and get them patented, produced, and sold. The U.S. patent system provides inventors with powerful rights with regard to inventions, but inventors must be willing to learn how to take advantage of the system.

Partnerships

Most inventions undergo various milestones in the development process. An invention may go through a series of modifications, improvements, and upgrades before a final concept or design is established and the product is ready to market. An inventor may substantially reduce the cost of development by teaming with partners who have proven expertise in patenting, marketing, and manufacturing. The inventor is likely to want to maintain control over certain aspects of the development process and team with partners who are capable of overseeing or assisting with the remaining aspects of the invention.

Design and Development

The main objective of designing and developing an invention extends beyond getting a patent issued. A patent only represents one aspect of attaining success with an invention. Design and development should have long-term implications, meaning the inventor must be capable of designing and developing inventions that will be used for a long time. Inventors, engineers, and product developers share the same primary objectives with respect to developing inventions. The design and development process must center on the following four primary objectives.

1) To Make Money

A monetary reward is the most popular return that inventors seek for their creative efforts. An inventor must incorporate methods of determining the money-making potential of the invention. The design, development, manufacture, and patent of an invention does not necessarily equate to generating royalties or profits. The invention must be sold to generate money. The sales potential of an invention should be measured using the three economic principles of need or desire, price point, and market size.

There must be a need or a desire for the invention. Need usually results in higher sales volume than desire. Need includes such things as food, shelter, and clothing. Desire is more concerned with the newest, most modern, or most luxurious. Since most people are capable of satisfying their basic needs, the driving principle behind most inventions is satisfying the psychological desires of the consumer. The design and development of an invention should address certain customer-driven innovation (CDI) factors. The invention should have a number of the following characteristics:

•	Offer a benefit to mankind.	•	Save time, space, and money.
•	Offer safety.	•	Offer convenience.
•	Offer comfort.	•	Provide entertainment.
•	Be user friendly or easy to learn.	•	Appeal to the senses.
•	Appeal to vanity.	•	Improve productivity.
•	Be incorporable to other systems.	•	Be user friendly.

The inventor capable of filling a void with an environmentally friendly invention, for example, will gain a market advantage. Price point has to do with developing an invention and evaluating the sale price relative to similar products already in the marketplace. During the development phase, an inventor should determine whether the invention will compete in the marketplace where branded products exist that consumers have confidence in and are comfortable with. The inventor must successfully compete in or monopolize this market. Many new products have successfully sold at premium prices, but as volume and competition increased, those prices tended to decline. Some product industries have little price elasticity so that a premium price may not be achievable, resulting in low profits or no market potential. Market size is a measure of the amount of the market that an invention may capture. A percentage-wise market niche may sound impressive, but if it represents only a small sum of money, the invention may not be cost effective. An 8 percent market niche, for example, may seem impressive until the numbers are figured and the 8 percent niche represents only $100,000 per year. This may be enough sales to justify the cost of developing the invention. Durability must also be computed. Whether the invention sustains years of stability or growth or whether it quickly falls victim to design-around is an issue that patent protection should address, but patent protection must be broadly implemented to ensure such protection.

2) To Secure the Future

A patented invention can offer enough return on investment to secure an inventor and his or her company far into the future. After a patent is issued, the government guarantees the inventor or his or her company, the legal right to monopolize the manufacture, sale, and use of the patented invention. An inventor must first be capable of acquiring a patent and assuring that it provides broad enough coverage to protect the invention from potential competitors. The inventor must then determine whether the expense of patenting the invention with adequate coverage and protection is justified by the sales potential of the invention, usually requiring the services of an expert patent attorney. The inventor must develop a response to competition and a strategy for selling licenses, if that is the goal. The inventor must also determine whether the invention represents a short-term fad or a long-term product worth the cost of patenting. Long-term trends, of course, are preferable.

There are other limitations to weigh, such as purchasing raw materials or components, obtaining other technology, licensing other technologies, overcoming environmental or safety hazards, and determining the best method of dealing with them, if they are applicable to the invention.

3) To Become a Leader in a Niche or Field

With patent protection an inventor can overcome competition and can create a niche and new opportunities in the niche. The original patent owner who understands the particular industry's niche, patents in that field, and patent laws, in general, is put in the unique position of acquiring patents more easily for new improvements to a patented invention. The inventor must maintain knowledge in the field and be willing to invest the necessary time and expense to gain such knowledge from various resources and put that knowledge to use.

4) To Have Fun

The design and development of an invention should offer some fun or satisfaction so the inventor maintains interest and drive to continue efforts and achieve long-term profits.

Documentation

A valid patent application must include specifics that adequately describe the invention and its preferred embodiments. The application should contain documented drawings with details about each component and how the invention works or is made.

Patent protection requires that the inventor or invention owner provide proof of how and when the invention was conceived and built. The necessary proof includes documentation of the invention's development, oftentimes provided on hand-written notes. Documentation should include dates and events relevant to the conception, construction, and development of the invention. During each stage of invention, development, notes, and sketches should be maintained to document the processes or objects.

Documentation becomes important legal evidence when establishing proof of conception, reduction to practice, rights of ownership, or arguing originality as compared to prior art references. Documentation should be made with a pen or a permanent marking device rather than a pencil or erasable marking device. Mistakes and modifications should be crossed out rather than erased. Such written documentation offers authenticity in developing a legally admissible patent application. Notes and documentation should be reviewed by a trusted outside source. That source should date and sign documents to indicate the existence of the documentation at the particular time indicated.

Written documentation provides a history of the invention, a disclosure of the invention, evidence of the date of conception, evidence of the date of practice, an organized set of milestones to authenticate when and how the invention was developed, and proof of business activities for tax purposes.

Biz Wiz Says . . . As an attorney, one of the things I like to see an inventor bring to my office is a notebook detailing his or her development of the invention. As will be discussed below, this is one of the simplest things an inventor can do to help prove their development of the invention.

Proof of Conception

Conception involves the intellectual side of an invention. Proof of conception requires that the inventor define how the invention was formulated or how the invention was intended to solve a problem.

Proof of Reduction to Practice

Reduction to practice is the conversion of the conception to a workable invention. The inventor must demonstrate that the invention actually works to serve its intended purpose. Such demonstration involves either an actual reduction to practice or a constructive reduction to practice. Actually building and testing the invention creates an actual reduction to practice. Submitting either a provisional or non-provisional patent application creates a constructive reduction to practice. The chosen application must describe how to make and use the invention and also demonstrate that the invention works.

Right of Ownership

Right of ownership is the establishment of ownership when more than one inventor conceives the same invention, when more than one person is involved in the development of an invention, or an invention is developed under an employer-employee relationship. When more than one inventor conceives of the same invention, documentation will assist in establishing which of them is the first true inventor. When more than one party is responsible for the development of an invention, documentation will assist in determining which parties are responsible for the various aspects of an invention. Documentation will also assist in resolving issues of ownership when the invention is developed under an employer-employee relationship.

Originality

The originality of an invention may be challenged by prior-art references that may include other patents, other publications, prior public knowledge, or prior public use of the invention. Prior-art references cannot be used against a patent application if documentation specifies the following:

- The invention was built and tested or a provisional patent application (PPA) was filed prior to the prior-art references' effective date.

- The invention was conceived prior to the prior-art reference's effective date and the invention was built and tested or some form of patent application was filed before the prior-art reference date.

Taxable Business Activity

The business of developing an invention qualifies as a business activity for tax purposes. The IRS qualifies inventing as a business activity if the primary reason for inventing is to earn profits and the individual engages in inventing activities regularly and continually over a period of time. As such, business expenditures incurred for inventing are deductible from ordinary income. The IRS expects that such deductions be supported by clear and accurate documentation that details the individual's invention activities, including conception, building, and testing the invention as well as expenditures for such activities.

The Lab Notebook

The most reliable and useful form of invention documentation is a permanently bound lab notebook with consecutively numbered pages. Specialty book and supply stores offer such notebooks designed to allow for drawings, sketches, photos, descriptions, notes, documentation, and signatures with dates for both inventors and their witnesses. However, any type of bound notebook is suitable so long as pages are consecutively numbered with appropriate dates and signatures. The ideal lab notebook will include the following components:

- A description of the invention and its novel features.
- Any additional documentation, such as approvals, correspondence, and purchase receipts.
- Drawings, photos, or sketches of the invention.
- Procedures necessary to build and test the invention.

- Expected test results and conclusions.
- A discussion of any known prior-art references.

The notebook should contain handwritten entries that accurately describe the events leading up to development. All entries should be signed and dated with an explanation for any delays in making appropriate entries. When it is not possible to include handwritten entries, such as with computer printouts, or photos, these external items should be affixed to the lab notebook, in chronological order, with a permanent adhesive. External items should be signed, dated, and affixed with descriptive documentation entered on the notebook page. To indicate that external items have not been substituted, lead lines should be drawn from and onto the external item to the page of the notebook. When an external item consumes the entire page of the notebook, documentation for that item should be referenced on an adjacent page, not the back of the page. Sketches and other external items that were originally created in pencil or other erasable marking device should be photocopied and affixed along with other external entries as described above.

All notebook entries should bear the witness's signature on the page. The witness should be capable of reading and understanding the subject matter being witnessed. One witness is sufficient for documentation purposes, but more than one witness increases the odds of having at least one of them available for testimony in court proceedings, if needed. If called upon to testify, the witness must be willing to attest to qualifications and the expertise necessary to interpret the technical aspects of the invention.

Witness signatures should not be equated with confidentiality. When a lab notebook contains confidential information that may be used in trade secrets, the documentation should clearly state that the information is confidential. A statement similar to "The above confidential information is witnessed and understood" should be documented on the same page of the notebook where the confidential information is entered or affixed. By witnessing and providing a witness signature to confidential entries in the lab notebook, the witness makes no commitment to confidentiality. To ensure the confidentiality of entries that may later need to be protected by trade secrets, the inventor must engage the witness in a separate and signed confidentiality agreement. It should be noted that a confidentiality agreement alone might not protect confidential information in a legal dispute with a signatory witness. The inventor must also be capable of proving that reasonable steps were taken to protect confidential information and that the information was not otherwise made public or available to an outside party.

Invention Disclosure

As an alternative to a lab notebook, an inventor may document the development of an invention using an Invention Disclosure form. An Invention Disclosure form may be used to document conception, building and testing of an invention. If any of these events occurs at a different time, separate disclosure forms must be completed. Each Invention Disclosure form must be signed and dated by the inventor and preferably two witnesses.

Disclosure Document Program (DDP)

The PTO offers a Disclosure Document Program (DDP) that allows an inventor to document the conception of the invention. Unlike an Invention Disclosure form, a disclosure document does not require witness signatures to validate the conception. An inventor must file a patent application based on the disclosure document within two years of filling the disclosure document because the PTO destroys all disclosure documents after two years. The filing of a disclosure document for a conception under the DDP does not relieve the inventor of the responsibility to document all events that apply to building and testing the invention in a lab notebook or through the use of a provisional patent application. The DDP only relieves the inventor of having to acquire expert witnesses to the conception of an invention.

To file a disclosure document under the DDP, the inventor sends the PTO a signed disclosure document along with a cover letter, a check for $10 to cover the processing fee, and a stamped self-addressed postcard. Disclosure documents may also be filed at select Patent and Trademark Depository Libraries (PTDLs). A copy of the disclosure will be maintained at the PTDL, while the original copy is sent to the PTO. Appropriate fees must be submitted with the disclosure so that it will be processed and retained by the PTO. The date of receipt at the PTO or PTDL has no bearing on date of filing application for any subsequently filed patent application.

A disclosure document must be submitted on white paper, no larger than 8½ by 11 inches, with numbered pages. All text and drawings must be sufficiently dark to allow for photocopying with typical copying machines. Oversized papers, videotapes, and models will not be accepted, but returned to the sender. The original document will not be returned; instead, the PTO will send the applicant a notice with an identifying number for the disclosure and the date of receipt at the PTO.

Ownership

Determining ownership of an invention means revealing who actually contributed to the concept, made suggestions for the design, and refined or improved the prototype. A patent may be issued to a sole owner or to multiple owners. Multiple owners usually include those individuals who contributed to the development of the invention. An IP professional may be sought to assist and advise on the complicated issue of multiple ownership.

Protection

The inventor or owner of an invention must determine whether the invention is best protected by a patent and whether it meets the qualifications for a patent. If it is determined that a patent is not a feasible choice, alternative methods of protection made be used that cost less and take less time than seeking patent protection.

If the invention involves a chemical, process, or improvement that does not require public exposure and it is possible for it to be contained within the company, establishing trade secrets offers the best form of protection.

Marketability

Determining the marketability of an invention will assist in justifying the amount of time, resources, and money to invest in an invention. Without assessing marketability, the inventor must guess the potential of the invention. Potential partners are not likely to invest in a guessing scheme but require factual data that indicate a potential for success. Marketability involves assessing and identifying attributes of the invention that provide a competitive edge in the marketplace. Determining marketability involves seeking trends, examining competitive responses, or evaluating state-of-the-art positioning.

Prototypes

The inventor, generally, needs to have a clear indication of the marketability and manufacturing process necessary for the invention before a final prototype of the invention is developed. In some situations, however, prototypes are developed concurrently with marketing and manufacturing processes. Some method of cost analysis is necessary to indicate the sufficiency of such processes. The prototype development process includes five phases, as follows.

- **Phase 1—A simple, crude model.** During this phase of prototyping an invention, the inventor gets a feel for the shape, size, and basic design of the invention. At this point, the prototype may be either nonfunctional or crudely functional. The prototype does not need to be made of the final desired materials. For example, it may be made of cardboard, carved in balsa wood, or molded from clay. Many inventors initiate the development of a prototype with the purchase of a similar product and then modify the product to reflect their invention. Inventors may form a prototype from a block of plastic or they may carve the prototype in wood and paint it with chrome paint to simulate steel. Others may use computer-generated graphics to illustrate a simple or crude prototype. If the invention is an electronic device, the general shape may be carved out of balsa wood or a plastic block with wiring extended to functioning electronics in a separate box. At this stage of development, the wiring and electronics are not expected to be neatly presented.

- **Phase 2—Testing functionality.** During this phase, the prototype should be less crude. It should be built from the final and desired materials and more closely resemble the final invention. Testing should be vigorous, irrespective of redundancy. The inventor should attempt to validate the final product and its appearance with marketing experts or others in field of the invention. Disclosure of the invention to such experts should be made with a confidentiality agreement.

- **Phase 3—Incorporating improvements.** Improvements that are necessary to correct failures and shortcomings evidenced by testing during Phase 2 should be implemented during this phase. In addition to improvements, sex appeal and dazzle should be added. At this phase, the prototype should be good enough to present to others in the industry, marketing experts, and prospective buyers. As such, the Phase 3 prototype should be sufficient and useful in attempts to secure marketing partners or attempts to get order commitments. From this stage forward, the inventor may want to partner with manufacturing and marketing experts to ensure that the prototype is properly presented with all of its attributes. Testing should be done in a test environment with end users. Observations of the testing should include critics of the functionality and both positive and negative responses of the end users.

- **Phase 4—A working prototype.** During this phase, a true working prototype from a test mold or an actual manufacturing process should be built and tested by end users. The inventor and marketing expert should be present for the testing and devise a system of receiving feedback from the users. The feedback and observations of responses from the users should be used to evaluate opinions and determine whether any final improvements and alterations are necessary.

- **Phase 5—The final prototype.** The final and production model should be complete during this stage and used substantially in test markets. Several test applications in different locations should be executed, providing the end user with the option of purchasing the product.

Manufacturing

The inventor must decide whether he or she is going to manufacture and distribute the invention or allow **another party to do so.** If another party is chosen, the inventor must decide which companies to approach based on research of prospective companies. Potential companies should be experienced in the particular field of the invention, be located near the inventor, and be producing items that the inventor is comfortable with. The inventor should decide whether a large corporation or small company would be better. If the product will require consumer education, the inventor needs to choose a company that will commit to relevant advertising or other long-term marketing techniques. If the inventor chooses to manufacture his or her own invention, a good understanding of manufacturing processes is necessary to ensure that the chosen process is cost-effective. In addition to being cost-effective, the chosen manufacturing process should be more desirable than existing, competitive products. In figuring manufacturing costs, the inventor-manufacturer needs to include the cost to produce, store, and distribute the product.

Ongoing Research and Evaluation

After an invention is designed, developed, manufactured, patented, and sold, the inventor must continue to engage in ongoing research and development in the field of the invention. Once an invention is on the market, competitors will attempt to gain a portion of the market share. Some competitors will attempt to design around the invention or develop a new competitive invention or offer new inventions at a lower cost. Others may attempt to infringe on the patented invention. In any case, the inventor will need to keep pace with what's going on in the marketplace and assess the patented invention against the market. New initiatives will have to be undertaken to continue to reap profits or maintain a niche in the market. New initiatives may include pursuing and patenting new improvements, starting a new business or new product line, or licensing the invention. The inventor will need to assess the potential of each initiative to determine what type and how many resources to commit to such initiatives. Ongoing research

Biz Wiz Says . . . During all stages of prototype development, the importance of confidentiality cannot be stressed enough. Merely disclosing the invention to another party without a confidentially agreement or nondisclosure agreement can adversely affect your rights.

and evaluation will allow the inventor to stay current with distributors and customers willing to purchase the invention, companies interested in using or marketing the invention and companies to target for licensing, manufacture, and sales.

chapter three

Intellectual Property (IP)

Some form of intellect must be used to create or develop an invention. That intellect is considered intellectual property (IP), an intangible creation of the mind that can be legally protected. It is not a physical object. IP has two components: assets and rights. IP assets are the physical or tangible creations developed from IP. IP rights are the legal protections that secure IP assets, including copyrights, trademarks, patents, trade secrets, and semiconductor mask works. The PTO is the government's expert authority on IP rights and assets. The PTO advises and assists other government agencies as well as other divisions of the Department of Commerce on issues regarding IP.

Types of IP Assets

As creations of the mind, IP assets may include just about anything imaginable. Inventions, expressions of art, product innovations, manufacturing method innovations, logos, commercial names, software, manuals, and promotional literature represent just a few IP assets. Though IP laws can protect all IP assets, not all IP assets meet the requirements to secure protection under patent laws. Patent rights provide protection for only a subset of IP assets, namely inventions. Other types of IP rights may protect other types of IP assets. The PTO issues patents for inventions based on several criteria, the most important of which are that the invention must be new, useful, and operable. An invention cannot be patented if the invention existed previously.

IP Assets That Cannot Be Patented

Patents may be sought for just about every type of invention, but patents are not issued for inventions that may be classified as perpetual motion machines or ideas. The PTO considers perpetual motion machines to be the impossible, and thus, not patentable. Likewise, the PTO issues patents based on the specified and documented design of a product or process. The invention must operate according to specifications that are defined and documented in the patent application. An idea or suggestion without design specifications cannot be patented.

Intellectual property rights are a legal matter that extends from the U.S. Constitution, Article 1, section 8, which mandates the U.S. Congress to "promote the progress of science and useful arts, by securing, for limited times, to authors and inventors, the exclusive right to their respective writings and discoveries."

One or more of the following Intellectual Property rights may be used to protect IP assets:

- Copyright – protects an artistic expression.
- Trademark – protects a brand name.
- Patent – protects an invention.
- Trade Secret – protects a formula or process.

Copyright and trademark laws attach themselves to IP assets as soon as the asset is created or used. However, they must be registered to claim ownership and have that ownership documented for legal purposes. Patent and Trade Secrets law, on the other hand, are not automatically attached to IP assets. Very specific procedures must be followed to protect IP assets, using these rights, requiring a hefty fee be paid to secure such protection.

In addition to protecting IP assets with IP rights, the government protects business entities from unethical businesses' taking advantage of unfair competition laws.

Copyright Laws

Copyrights are the most easily acquired and understood intellectual property (IP) rights. Fundamental laws regulating copyrights are as defined by Title 17 of the U.S. Code—The Copyright Act. They are regulated by the federal government and exercised in the federal court system. State and local jurisdictions have no authority to arbitrate copyright issues. Copyright laws, like patent laws, provide the legal right to protect an invention, but copyright laws do not protect abstractions, technical concepts, or functional concepts. Copyright laws protect an original work of authorship (OWA), which may include such things as text, a graphic, music, a literary work, a video production, or a sculpture. A copyright provides offensive rights for an author's particular way of expressing work. By default, these types of works or inventions are protected by copyright laws as soon as they are created. However, should another party dispute the originality of the work, some proof of authorship of the creation must be submitted by making application to register a copyright of the work with the U.S. Copyright Office of the Library of Congress. The application must include a copy of the work as proof of authorship.

A copyright protects the form of an expression, not a subject matter. A copyright will not protect a phrase, idea, method, process, concept, principle, form, system, plan, or device. A separability requirement dictates that a copyright may not be used for a utilitarian article unless it has an aesthetic feature that can exist independently of the article or can be separated from the article. As an example, a copyright may protect a design on a baseball bat because the design is an aesthetic feature that may exist independent of the bat, but the bat itself is a utilitarian article that cannot be copyrighted because the design of the bat cannot be separated from the bat.

The law does not require that copyrights be registered to receive protection. If registration is completed within three months of distribution, publication, or infringement of a work, the owner is entitled to receive costs, damages, and attorney fees as statutory damages in an infringement lawsuit. Statutory damages may be awarded without proof. Though it is not required, it is advisable to include a notice with copyrighted work that indicates that work is indeed covered by copyright laws. A copyright notice that makes use of the symbol, ©, when properly placed, indicates the owner of the copyright and when the work was first published. The notice prevents an infringer from claiming that the infringement was accidental.

Trademark Laws

Trademark laws are unique in that they protect brand names, designs, or other symbols that are used to identify or market goods and services. Trademark laws prevent another party from using the same mark or a similar mark when it is easily confused with an established mark. Trademarks will not prevent another party from making the same product or selling the same product under a different and non-confusing mark. When the same or similar mark is used to tarnish the image of an established trademark, the owner of the established trademark may sue for infringement. Even in situations where a newly established mark is used to promote goods or services that are in no way similar to the goods or product being protected by the established trademark, the owner of the established trademark may sue for infringement. Like copyrights, trademarks attach to IP assets as soon as they are created. The protection provided by trademarks does not require that the trademark be registered. As with copyrights, the registration of trademarks validates ownership in the case of disputes. Protection is provided to the first person to make use of a trademark in commerce or the first person to file an intent-to-use application for a trademark and then actually use the trademark in commerce. To make use of a trademark in commerce, an individual must use the trademark name in advertisements, shipping, or labeling in interstate or foreign commerce.

Before investing money marketing and disseminating the name of a product, perform a trademark search or have one performed by a search firm. The U.S. Patent and Trademark Office Web site allows a search of all issued trademarks and trademark applications. It is a good place to start.

Patent Laws

A patent provides the legal right to protect inventions that represent either mental concepts or creations. Patent laws specify the subject matter that may be patented and the conditions under which a patent may be issued. A patent protects any new mental concept or creation that provides for a useful process, machine, manufacture, composition of matter, or any new use of such inventions or discoveries. As such, a patent may protect virtually anything made by man as well as the processes by which such things are made so long as certain conditions are met. A process is defined as any method or act, but a patentable process is primarily concerned with industrial and technical methods or acts. A manufacture is any made or manufactured article, inclusive of mixtures of ingredients and new chemical compounds. A composition of matter includes matter in any state: gas, liquid, or solid.

The latest patent law modifications ensure that every pending patent application filed as of the November 29, 2000, is published for public viewing 18 months after the application filing date except when the applicant indicates that the patent will not be filed abroad. The advantage of making application for a patent is that an infringer may be sued for royalties if the patent is later issued. Such royalties are assessed and paid from the date of publication. The law also requires that the infringer must have had notice of the publication. The inventor or invention owner need only send the infringer a copy of the publication to meet this requirement. The law allows a patent application to be published even if it is later rejected for the issuance of a patent. Unfortunately, the inventor or invention owner risks losing both trade secret rights and patent rights as a result of the publication. The applicant may withdraw the patent application before publication to prevent the release of confidential information that would otherwise be protected by trade secret laws.

A patent is a form of personal property that may be sold for cash, licensed for royalties or transferred in ownership. A patent may be transferred from one party to another as a gift, by will or by descent. When a deceased patent owner has no established will, patents transfer as specified by the particular state's intestate succession laws. The main court to handle patent issues is the Court of Appeals for the Federal Circuit Court (CAFCC).

Trade Secret Laws

Trade secret laws are used to protect formulas, manufacturing processes, or other commercially advantageous materials. Commercially advantageous materials include information that is not generally known and gives a business its competitive edge. In order to make use of the rights afforded by trade secret laws, a strategy and policy must be implemented to ensure that information is disseminated to only those individuals with a need to know. Some materials, despite careful strategic methods and policies, are not practical to secure and must be protected using other types of IP rights.

Though companies are required to take only reasonable precautions to keep their company trade secrets confidential, companies must expend great amounts of time, money, and resources to guard their trade secrets from competitors. The federal government and most states have statutes that make theft of a trade secret both a criminal and civil offense. At the federal level, the theft of trade secrets is considered economic espionage.

Unfair Competition Laws

Unfair competition includes various devious and unfair methods of advertisement, marketing, endorsement, packaging, and promotion. Unfair competition laws change frequently. New rulings have been known to contradict established laws. A business entity that chooses to exercise such laws must be up-to-date in the latest appropriate rulings. In a proven case of unfair competition an injunction is issued which prohibits the violating business entity from continuing its activity. The injunction will also define future business practices of the violating business entity. The violating business entity may be required to pay compensation to the injured business to cover lost profits due to the unfair competition.

chapter four

Contractual IP Rights

IP rights such as copyrights and trademarks are automatically attached to certain IP assets, giving immediate protection to the creator of the asset. However, IP rights may also be extended to other than the creator. IP rights may be sold, leased, transferred, or assigned to another party.

Royalties

Contractual IP rights may be extended to another party for payment in the form of royalties. Royalties may be paid in return for a license to make or use an IP asset or right. Royalties provide for the owner of IP rights to collect a percentage of the proceeds from the sale and use of a creation by the other party.

Licensing

Licensing is a method of allowing the party with existing IP rights to lease those rights to another party or to allow another party to make use of the acquired IP rights for a profit. A license is a contract between two parties, the licensee and the licensor. The licensor owns the IP asset and its associated rights. The licensee is the entity that makes use of the IP asset or the IP rights in exchange for the payment of royalties or some other agreed upon consideration of value. If the licensor owns an IP asset that is an invention, the right to the invention is as held by a patent. The licensee may make use of the invention in exchange for the payment of royalties or other consideration to the licensor. The licensee is permitted use of the invention without consequence of being sued for infringing upon the patent rights of the invention. A license differs from an assignment, which transfers an asset as well as rights to the asset. A license does not transfer an asset or the right of the asset; a license gives the licensee permission to use the asset only. In return for the agreed upon payment, the licensor may not cancel the licensee's authorization to make use of the asset. As such, a license is equivalent to a property lease in which the landlord gives the tenant permission to use a property for living space so long as required rent payments are made on time. Leasing property is very different from selling property just as licensing a patent right or asset is very different from assigning a patent right or asset.

An inventor maintains ownership of a patented invention throughout the life of the invention unless the inventor assigns those rights to another party. When an inventor licenses a patented invention, the licensee may require the inventor to sign a waiver relinquishing certain rights to the invention. Larger corporations may require that the inventor waive all rights except patent rights. Smaller companies may require less stringent waivers and some may not require a waiver at all.

Types of Licenses

The type of license that may be offered by a licensor is dependent on the type of IP right that protects the IP asset. There are six types of licenses that may be offered. They include the following:

Patent License

A patent license permits a licensee to make use of one of three IP assets. They include a technological breakthrough, also known as an improvement, an ornamental design and a plant variety. Note that in legal and licensing documentation, a technological breakthrough is termed an improvement rather than a patent. IP assets may be licensed before they are patented because a license is a contract, which is independent from any patent that may be licensed. When a licensee acquires a license for an invention, the licensee is buying insurance against being sued for patent infringement when and if the invention is patented. If the invention is never patented, the licensee is still obligated to pay royalties for the duration of the license contract.

Trade-Secret License

A trade secret license contractually obligates the licensor to disclose proprietary and confidential information to the licensee in exchange for payment. It also obligates the licensee to keep the supplied information confidential. This type of license agreement is commonplace in the chemical industry. Chemical formula and compositions are relatively easy to keep confidential, and a trade license agreement is often more practical than acquiring a patent.

Copyright License

A copyright license provides a licensee with right to make use of one or more copyrighted works. A copyright license may be sold even when the licensor fails to register the copyright with the PTO, but registration is encouraged to offer a broader scope of protection.

Trademark/Service-Mark License

A trademark or service mark license authorizes the licensee to operate a business under one or more of the licensor's commercial identifiers. The licensor then obligates himself or herself to maintain some type of quality control over the business activities of the licensee to maintain the reputation that the identifier has enjoyed. Many of the products offered for sale in the U.S. are manufactured under both foreign and domestic licensees. The U.S. does not require that marks be registered before licenses are sold, but it is highly recommended. In foreign nations that do not conform to first use rules in commerce, mark registration is required. First use rules are discussed under "Protecting a Patent—Foreign Applicants for U.S. Patents." Registration consists of obtaining entry on the particular foreign government's registry where first rights are assigned in order of entry in the registry.

Merchandising License

A merchandising license can be a copyright, trademark, or a combination of a trademark and copyright license. A merchandising license extends the range of goods protected by copyrights and trademarks beyond their original purposes. A merchandising license provides for the rental of commercial identifiers for use on a variety of goods and services. As such, a merchandising license provides for name exploitation based on the value of the commercial identifier and the impression it gives. Exploitation of the name signifies nothing about the quality or reputation of the product nor does it signify anything about the service originally provided under the mark.

Combination License

Combination licenses allow a number of IP assets and rights to be bundled together. This type of license has application in situations such as when a licensee is licensed to produce and sell a patented article under the licensor's mark and also to package the article with copyrighted graphics. A combination license may be acquired, subject to antitrust prohibitions.

When a contractual agreement to license IP rights and assets is entered, the contract must clearly define the rights or asset being licensed. A clause must also be included to define the scope of permitted activities. This clause is considered to be the most important part of a license agreement. As such, a license agreement includes basic clauses, and it must also include clauses specific to a company's business processes, such as future improvements, technical assistance, warranties, notices, termination, arbitration, legal action against infringers, and legal fees. Though it is not required, a licensee is encouraged to seek the professional services of a competent IP professional to negotiate or draft a suitable license agreement.

Franchising

Franchising is a method of transferring existing IP rights to another party. A franchise is a trademark or service mark license with established rules about how the licensee (franchisee) shall conduct business under the name of the franchise. Business is to be conducted according to methods imposed by the licensor (franchisor). A franchise usually requires that the franchisor transfer knowledge and technical assistance as part of the contractual agreement. The franchisee is usually required to advance the franchisor a large down payment in exchange for the right to operate under the franchisor's service mark. Franchisees are bound to operate according to established methods and under strict quality control. Some franchisors also institute operating controls to ensure that franchises operate in compliance with necessary and applicable state and federal regulations.

Assignments

Assignment is a method of selling existing IP rights to another party. A patent assignment is a legal document that transfers property ownership. It must be notarized or acknowledged by a U.S. consular officer, if parties to the assignment are abroad. The language of an assignment must clearly indicate what is being assigned in complete and readily identifiable form. A copy or photograph of the assigned property should be included in the assignment agreement. After a patent assignment is recorded with the PTO, the recording prevents the transferor from assigning the patent to another party. If a patent or patent application assignment is not recorded within three months of providing signatures to the assignment, any subsequent assignment that is recorded takes precedence over the unrecorded assignment. Payment for an assignment should be established in the same fashion as lump-sum or royalty payments for licenses, as described above under "Licensing."

Elements of a License

Exclusivity

An exclusivity clause must be included to determine who is to make use of a licensed invention. If an agreement is exclusive, the licensor waives all rights to make or practice the invention or to license it to another party. If an agreement is co-exclusive, the licensor retains the right to practice the invention, but agrees not to license it to anyone except the licensee. If an agreement is non-exclusive, the licensor retains the right to practice the invention and also license it to third parties who are in competition with the licensee.

An exclusivity clause also determines the amount of royalty

payments to be paid and legal rights of the parties to the agreement. Most license agreements provide for higher royalties for exclusive licenses than are required for co-exclusive and non-exclusive licenses. Also, exclusive licensees are entitled to file legal action against infringers whereas co-exclusive and non-exclusive licensees are not.

Field of Use

A licensor, as owner of IP assets and IP rights, may parcel the geographical area and commercial field in which the licensee may practice or apply an invention. The type of exclusivity acquired with a license may be used to define the territory or field of use. A non-exclusive license may offer the licensee a more restrictive field of use than an exclusive license.

Life Span

The life of a license agreement must be no longer than the life of the IP right being licensed. In the case of patents, the life of a license agreement must be no longer than the 20 years, for utility and plant patents and 14 years for design patents.

Payment and Remuneration

Payment for a license to practice an invention may be made in lump sums, royalties that are based on an agreed upon parameter or a combination of both. Royalties may be based on such things as net proceeds, cost of goods, number of items sold, or other circumstances of the particular business entity, such as anticipated sales, investment dollars and the financial status of the business. When royalty rates are based on parameters that are determined by circumstances of the business payments, delayed payments, variable royalty rates and guaranteed payments must be clearly specified in the license agreement. When a license agreement is exclusive, the licensor must rely upon the licensee's ability to exploit the licensed IP asset. As such, the license agreement should include a minimum performance clause that obligates the licensee to achieve a certain level of performance. The minimum performance amount may be calculated on a sliding scale or some other agreed upon performance system.

Reporting

The licensee should be required to provide the licensor with periodic reports of the sales and income of the business unit applicable to the license. Reporting allows the licensor to monitor the progress of the licensee, particularly when license fees are not paid in lump sum and the licensee is committed to a payment schedule.

Control

If the licensee is operating under the mark of the licensor, a clause specifying the quality of goods or services to be offered for sale under the mark must be included in the license agreement. The licensor is liable for any losses incurred as a result of poor or inadequate service and failure or defect of a product. A patent license agreement is not likely to make any warranty as to the worth of an invention, nor will it guarantee that an invention will work as expected or that a process is safe or effective. The licensor is not legally obligated to exert any form of quality control over the business activities of the licensee. As such, the licensor is not liable for any loss due the failures or misdeeds attributable to the licensee.

Biz Wiz Says...

Patent licenses are typically complex legal agreements and the assistance of an attorney is recommended.

Recording a License

In general, the government does not require that license agreements be filed or registered with any type of regulatory agency. However, governments do establish methods of recording the transfer of titles and assignments of property as official notice that such transactions have taken place. Patent and trademark license agreements may be recorded with the PTO. Likewise copyright licenses may be recorded with the Copyright Office. Any license agreement, particularly an exclusive license agreement, warrants a recording of the license to make notice of the transfer of rights, deter infringers from infringing and prevent the licensor from selling the license to another party.

A franchise license is an exception to the rule since franchises do require government approval. Most states require that a franchise "qualify" for state approval. To qualify for approval, a franchisor must disclose its franchising scheme and indicate an ability to fulfill the promises of any proposed license agreement. Some states impose very strict requirements on franchisors, and the qualification process may take months to complete. Upon qualification, the franchise must be recorded with appropriate state agencies. Franchising is a more complex form of licensing that may require the services of an IP professional that specializes in franchising and, preferably, in the particular field of art of the particular franchise, though there is no requirement to acquire such service.

Licenses and Taxes

Federal and state laws govern some types of licensing to make sure all applicable taxes are paid and that anti-trust laws are not violated. The licensing of IP assets and rights involves an exchange of money and income, which is subject to taxation by the government. Proceeds from the sale of licenses are usually considered to be ordinary income while proceeds from an assignment are considered to be capital gains. Each is taxed as such. U.S. tax laws provide that capital gains be taxed at a lower rate than ordinary income. The IRS may allow some exclusive patent licenses to be treated as assignments in situations where the licensor relinquishes all or most control of the licensed IP asset. In the issuance of licenses, proceeds from lump-sum and royalty payments on the sale or exchange of a patent are considered to be long-term capital gains for tax purposes. In negotiating the transfer of IP rights and assets, the licensor may want to consider the tax consequences of transaction. Licensors may find it to be more cost-effective to engage in an assignment rather than a license after tax considerations have been applied to the transaction. Taxation can be a complicated issue that may require the expert services of a tax attorney or Certified Public Accountant (CPA) though there is no requirement to engage such services.

License Legalities

In some sense, copyrights, patents, and trademarks are monopolies that are offered in exception to antitrust and unfair competition regulations. As such, courts and government agencies monitor their use to prevent owners of IP rights from engaging in coercive practices. IP owners, who attempt to leverage IP rights to obtain advantages that are not directly related to established IP rights, may incur problems. Two of the most common coercive practices include tie-ins and bundling.

Tie-ins

A tie-in is the illegal act of obligating a licensee to purchase something that is beyond the scope of the licensor's IP rights.

As an example, a licensor patents a printer and contractually obligates a licensee to purchase cartridges from him or her as well. However, patent rights are only applicable to the printer, not the printer cartridges. The licensee would be guilty of tie-in, based on the obligations of the license agreement to purchase printer cartridges. If, on the other hand, the licensee patented the printer and the only functional printer cartridge was also a sole-source product of the licensee, the licensee would be obligated to purchase printer cartridges from the licensee, by default, because the printer cartridges could not be acquired elsewhere. The contractual agreement would center on the quantity and timeliness of purchasing printer cartridges, but no illegal tie-in occurs.

Bundling

Bundling is not necessarily an illegal act, but more of a questionable act. Bundling occurs when a licensor engages in one of the following acts:

- Compels a licensee to accept licenses based on several different patents.
- Compels a licensee to accept licenses based on other IP rights.
- Bundles different IP assets or rights in a single license.
- Bundles different IP assets and rights in related licenses.

Bundling is questionable, rather then illegal, because the nature of a wrongful act is dependent upon the particular circumstances. Expanding on the printer example from above, a licensor patents a printer and contractually obligates a licensee to purchase cartridges as well. In this example, the licensor also patents the printer cartridge. However, the technology of the printer cartridge is available from other sources. The licensor would be in violation of anti-trust laws since the licensor is attempting to sole-source a product that is readily available in the market from other sources. If, on the other hand, the licensee's printer cartridge offers a superior design or functionality over competing printer cartridges, the licensor is not in violation of any anti-trust laws. Bundling also occurs when a patent licensor obligates a licensee to make use of the licensor's trademark. If, however, the licensee initiates the situation by requesting to license the trademark along with the patent, no questionable act occurs.

Losing IP Rights

While IP rights exist to protect IP assets, the United States is governed by antitrust and antimonopoly laws. As such, IP rights are issued with limitations and the penalty for misuse of those rights is forfeiture of the IP assets that IP rights were intended to protect.

IP Attorneys

Many businesses and corporate lawyers are willing to take on IP issues, but they may not be competent to handle IP issues. The PTO accredits registered IP attorneys and agents to represent companies and individuals in IP matters. Registered professionals have technical or scientific education or experience and must pass rigorous examinations relative to patent application procedures.

 **Biz Wiz Says . . .**

A list of registered patent attorneys is available at the U. S. Patent and Trademark Web site.

chapter five

Establishing Copyrights

Copyrights are established to protect an original work of authorship (OWA), which is defined as a substantial and fixed creative work of a non-technical character, originated by its author. By default, these types of works or inventions are protected by copyright laws as soon as they are created. However, they must be registered to document ownership. Copyrights do not protect abstractions nor technical or functional concepts.

Original Work of Authorship (OWA)

An original work is a work that isn't copied from an existing source. The work need not be new, innovative, or unusual. In fact, the work may have been created in another place, at some other time and by some other person, but the new author may not have been influenced by or exposed to the earlier work. A work that is based on or influenced by an existing work is termed a derivative work. A derivative work may only be used with the permission of the original author of the OWA. The new author may not obtain a copyright for the derivative work, but a copyright may be obtained if any part of the work is original. This is more easily said than interpreted.

The fundamental rule of copyrights is that copyrights define an expression of a work, not the idea behind the work. Take a copyrighted cookbook, for example. The recipes contained within the cookbook are functional processes that are not protected by copyright laws. It is the manner in which the recipes are presented and displayed that is protected by copyright. A new author may create a new cookbook using the same recipes but modify the format and sequence of steps. Copyright laws protect the mental intellect used to develop the new cookbook. If, on the other hand, the new author presented the recipes exactly as previously published, the new author would have to obtain permission from the original author to make use of the work. The new author cannot infringe on the copyright of the original work. The new author, however, may add additional design features, illustrations or text, which constitute original work that the new author may copyright.

As the name implies, an OWA must be an original work, but it must also meet certain other requirements to be copyrighted. It must:

- Be a fixed creation of the mind.
- Have significant complexity, scope, duration, or length.
- Not be primarily functional.

A fixed creation implies that the creation is in a tangible or reproducible state.

Copyright laws categorize OWAs into eight different types, dependent upon the type of work created. A work may fit into one or more of the categories or a work may be composed of several works that fall within different categories. The eight categories of an OWA include the following:

- Literary Works
- Musical Works
- Sound Recording Works

- Dramatic Works

- Motion Pictures and Audiovisual Works

- Architectural Works

- Pictorial, Graphic, and Sculptural Works

- Pantomimes and Choreographic Works

A music video, for example, may include several categories of work. It may contain a combination of musical, dramatic, audiovisual, and choreographic works.

Copyrights also protect two categories of work that don't meet the requirements to be considered OWAs.

1. Mask Works (for semiconductor chips).

2. Original Design of Useful Article Works.

Copyrights vs. Patent Protection

In general, inventions that are patentable are not copyrightable and vice versa. Patents provide protection for the functionality of an invention, abstraction, or concept while copyrightable works may not have such characteristics. Utility patents are issued to protect the functional aspects of an invention. Copyrightable works, by definition, are not functional. Confusion arises with new technological innovations, such as computer software. Computer software is composed of a series of numerical relationships or routines, which constitute a creative work of art, and thus, may be considered copyrightable. On the other hand, the series of routines is responsible for the functionality of the computer or associated hardware, which constitutes a utilitarian result, and thus, may be considered patentable under a utility patent. The choice of the type of protection is not clearly defined. The parties who are responsible for the software must weigh the benefit of offensive rights provided by the two types of protection. Though patents offer a broader range of offensive protection than do copyrights, copyrights are more easily obtainable with minimal cost and effort. In contrast, patents are expensive and time-consuming to obtain.

Both copyrights and design patents may be used to provide protection for aesthetics. However, design patents are used to protect industrial designs. Industrial designs are designs where the shape of the object is ornamental and not separable from the object. The tread of a tire, for example, represents an industrial design that remains affixed to the tire. A patent may protect the design of the tire tread. The striping for a vehicle, on the other hand, may be separated from the vehicle and may not be patented. However, it may be copyrighted.

Copyrights may be used in conjunction with patents to provide a broader range of offensive protection against infringers. A patent, for example, may be sought to protect a board game. The game pieces, directions, rules, and box design, however, offer no patentable attributes, but they may be protected by copyright laws. To provide even more offensive protection, the name of the game may be protected by trademark.

Copyright Limitations

Copyrights are intended to share the life of the work that it protects. In 1978 major changes were made to the Copyright Act, which extended the duration of a copyright based upon when the work was created and the nature of the authorship. When an employee creates a work on behalf of an employer or as an independent contractor, under a written "work-made-for-hire" contract, the work is considered a "work made for hire." The employer or the party who hires the contractor has ownership of the copyright even though the employee or contractor authors the work. For most works made for hire, the copyright extends 95 years from the date of publication or 120 years from the date of creation, whichever is shortest. Changes abolished the right to renew a copyright. Prior to 1978, a copyright had a duration of 17 years and could be renewed for an additional 28 years. New laws dictate that copyrights have durations as defined below in Table 1. All copyrights expire on the last day of the year of expiration.

DURATION OF COPYRIGHTS

Created On or After January 1st 1978	
Authorship	Duration
1 or more identified authors	Life of last surviving author plus 70 years
1 or more anonymous authors	The shorter of 95 years from publication or 120 years from work creation
Works made for hire	The shorter of 95 years from publication or 120 years from work creation
Created, but Not Published as of January 1st 1978 (No expiration prior to December 31, 2002)	
Authorship	Duration
1 or more identified authors	Life of last surviving author plus 70 years
1 or more anonymous authors	The shorter of 95 years from publication or 120 years from work creation
Works made for hire	The shorter of 95 years from publication or 120 years from work creation
Published after December 31, 1977, but before January 1· 2003 (No expiration prior to December 31, 2047)	
Authorship	Duration
One or more identified authors	Life of last surviving author plus 70 years
One or more anonymous authors	The shorter of 95 years from publication or 120 years from work creation
Works made for hire	The shorter of 95 years from publication or 120 years from work creation
Created and Published with Notice or Registered as of January 1st 1964, but before December 31st 1977	
Authorship	Duration
Any	The shortest of 95 years from publication or 95 years from registration

Created and Published with Notice or Registered as of January 1st 1950, but before December 31st 1963	
Authorship	Duration
Any renewed during the 28th year	The shortest of 95 years from publication or 95 years from registration
Any not renewed	The shortest of 28 years from publication or 28 years from registration

Table 1 - Duration of Copyrights

Defining Ownership

Issues of ownership are more prevalent when more than one party contributes to the development of an OWA. When the development of an OWA involves an employee-employer relationship or more than one associate, collaborator or contractor, the specifics of ownership must be clearly defined.

Making Application

For copyright laws protect a work authored by a U.S. citizen from infringement, the work must be registered. Because a copyright attaches itself to a work as soon as it is created, registration is not mandatory. The author of the work may or may not include the copyright mark with or on a work. If no one ever infringes on the copyrighted work, the registration becomes insignificant. If on the other hand, the author of a work is a U.S. citizen, another party does infringe on the copyright and the copyright has not been registered, the author has no right to bring an infringement action to the courts. Foreign residents are not required to register copyrights in the United States. An international treaty signed into agreement on March 1, 1989, the Berne Convention, prohibits included countries from imposing their own formalities upon foreign copyrights.

The United States is one such country.

Registering

It is a relatively simple process to register a copyright with the Copyright Office. The process includes filing an appropriate application, submitting materials that identify the work and paying the processing fee of about $45. A complete schedule of fees charged by the U.S. Copyright Office is shown at Appendix I. Once the application is received, the Copyright Office will provide one of following within three to six months.

- A stamped copy of the application that indicates proof of registration.

- A request for additional information or documentation.

- A letter of rejection with an indication of the reason for rejection.

Recording Documents

Any documents that indicate actions that affect a copyrighted work may be filed and recorded with the Copyright Office. Such recordings may include copyright assignments, court orders, license agreements, and other legal documents that are associated with the copyright. The recorded documents are made accessible to the public, and they provide constructive notice to viewers that the particular work is copyrighted.

Relinquishing Rights

Copyrights provide protection to the party that owns the right to the copyright. Copyright ownership may be relinquished only with the sale, transfer, or license of a fixed work to another party.

Sale and Transfer

To sell or transfer a copyrighted work to another party, the work must be in a tangible or reproducible state. In other words, the work must be fixed. The author of the work may sell or transfer copyright ownership of any part of the work that is fixed. When copyright ownership is divided amongst more than one party, each party holds an interest in the copyright and is entitled to sell or transfer that interest to another party. Copyright ownership of works or parts of works that are intended to be fixed in the future may not be sold or transferred.

Compulsory Licenses

Copyright laws dictate that copyrighted works include a compulsory license. A compulsory license forces the author of a work to grant permission non-voluntarily to the public to create derivatives of the copyrighted work. In return for the privilege, the third party is required to pay royalties for the use of the copyrighted work. The Copyright Office establishes a royalty panel that is responsible to determine rates for royalty payments.

Congress regularly introduces major revisions to the Copyright Act to account for advances in the music industry. The Internet and computer software that allow sharing of music pose a threat of extinction to the recording industry unless laws are enacted to legitimize electronic music sharing, which is now a violation of the Copyright Act. Critics indicate that some method should be implemented to compensate record companies with royalties from the sale of equipment to perform such acts or with royalties from sales generated by service providers that allow for the transmission of such music.

Licensing Musical Works

The sale, recording, and performance of musical works offer complexity in the licensing of copyrights. While copyrights are used to regulate the activity of creating musical work, the licensing of copyrights is used to regulate the distribution of such musical work. Permission may be granted to make use of musical works using three different types of licenses. Each type of license serves a unique purpose as follows:

- A mechanical license grants permission to reproduce a work.

- A performing license grants permission to use a work in a public performance.

- A synchronization license grants permission to broadcast a work, such as the background music used in a motion picture.

Associations of recording companies, songwriters, and music publishers have attempted to simplify the process of making agreements with the many record companies, radio stations, TV stations, theatres, and other business entities that either record, perform, or broadcast a work. These associations have established very complex, yet efficient methods of transferring copyrights and channeling a small percentage of mechanical and performing royalties back to the copyright owner.

Performing Licenses

Most of the proceeds acquired for copyrighted musical creations stem from the royalties paid on performing licenses. Associations of recording companies, songwriters, and music publishers offer memberships to songwriters and maintain a listing of all musical works created by members of the organization. The organization, not the individual members, engage in license agreements with theaters and broadcasting companies which obligate the licensee to monitor, report, and pay performing royalties. Songwriter organizations and author organizations then collect and distribute royalties each time a musical work is publicly performed or broadcast, such as on a radio station. The performance or broadcast may be either live or recorded. One half of the royalties are paid to the author/songwriter and the other half of the royalties are paid to music publishers who create the recording or publish the sheet music.

Music publishing companies collect one half of the performing royalties, and they also profit from proceeds from the mechanical licensing of recordings and sheet music as discussed below under "Mechanical Licenses." To prevent publishing companies from exploiting sales, many songwriters have created their own music publishing companies for the purpose of merging with other reputable publishing companies. The songwriter's ability to establish a sole proprietorship for the purpose of this type of merger is matter of formality in most states. The merger entitles both companies to share equally in the publisher's share of performance license royalties. Rather than receive only one half of the performing license royalties, the songwriter also receives, through his or her proprietorship, one half of the music publisher's 50 percent, for a total of 75 percent of performing license royalties. The merged music publisher is then entitled to the remaining 25 percent.

Mechanical Licenses

Mechanical licenses permit a company to record or publish a musical creation. Mechanical licenses may be either voluntary or compulsory. A voluntary license is negotiated and granted with a record company. The negotiation is relatively simple since royalty rates and modes of payment are standardized in the U.S. Most music publishing and recording companies offer a standard agreement, which provides the copyright owner with a small royalty payment for each record or piece of sheet music that is sold. The royalty payment is small since these companies must also bear the expenses of musicians, studio time and other activities associated with packaging and selling recordings.

Any recording company may claim a compulsory license after an author has authorized a company to produce or sell the recorded work. The Copyright Act, by default, dictates that a copyrighted work include a compulsory license. It also requires licensees of compulsory licenses to report sales to the copyright owner. Clearinghouses have been established to take on the cumbersome task of reporting such sales between music publishers and recording companies. The royalty rate and payment schedule used by these clearinghouses are standard and are usually lower than those established by the Copyright Office.

Synchronization Licenses

A synchronization license is issued when a musical work is synchronized with other sounds or images in a film or other recording medium. When a musical work is chosen for use as background music for a movie, video production, play, or other performance, the copyright owner is entitled to royalty payments for the use of the work. The industry makes use of a standard license agreement unless the copyright owner and producer establish a relationship that allows for a negotiated license agreement. Clearinghouses that are established to handle the reporting of sales for compulsory license royalties also handle the reporting of sales for synchronization licensing.

Exemptions to Copyright Infringement

Activities that would otherwise be considered infringement on a copyright are allowed for certain non-profits, charities, and for educational purposes.

Using the Copyright Mark

The copyright mark, ©, may be attached with or on a copyrighted works as soon as they are created. The copyright mark serves as legal notice to the viewer that the work is protected. It gives no indication as to whether the work is protected by a registered copyright. A copyright notice must include the following visible attributes:

- With the exception of sound recordings, the word Copyright, the abbreviation Copr, or the mark ©. Sound recordings use the mark, (P).

- Year of first publication.

- Identification of the copyright owner.

The © symbol is recognized by other countries as it is specified under the Universal Copyright Convention. A copyright notice should also indicate parts of a work that are excluded from copyright ownership. As an example, the notice, "©2006 John Doe excluding charts," is included in a copyrighted book. The notice indicates that charts included in the book are not protected by copyright. The referenced charts are publicly available from the government. Government publications are, by law, not copyrightable and may be freely copied and sold.

Researching an Existing Copyright

To make use of a copyrighted work, one may have to engage in research to locate the owner of the copyright. Even if the owner of the copyrighted work is identified, the owner may not be interested in granting permission to use the work without receiving monetary or some other form of compensation.

chapter six

Establishing Trademarks

A trademark may include a name, word, phrase, slogan, logo, shape, design, symbol, or other characteristic used to identify a product and distinguish it from other products. Any non-functional characteristic may be used to identify a product and serve as a trademark. Trademarks are often confused with trade names. A trademark is a word or other symbol that a company uses to sell its products or services. A trademark indicates the source or origin of a particular product or service and distinguishes it from other products and services. A trade name is a word or phrase under which a company does business. The trade name Procter & Gamble, for example, is the name of the company that sells, among other things, various brands of toothpaste under the trademark, Crest. In many instances, however, the trademark name and the company trade name are the same, thus, the confusion in terms. The trade name and trademark are commonly the same for newly established inventions that are developed, marketed, and manufactured by the same company. The name, Spic & Span, for example, is a commonly known trade name and trademark.

Commercial Identifiers

Commercial identifiers are a class of IP assets that uniquely identify a particular product, service, or company. A good commercial identifier positions a product or service in the marketplace. The distinctiveness and appeal of the identifier increases the chances of being able to protect, market, promote, and profit from the identifier. An identifier that gains strength and reputation in the marketplace becomes a valuable commodity that may be financially exploited. The primary roles of commercial identifiers include the following:

- To promote a product or service.

- To protect against copycatting and unfair appropriation of an established reputation or goodwill.

- To generate profit when exploited or traded.

There are three basic types of commercial identifiers, including the following:

- **Product Identifiers** — Brand names, which may be as simple as a design, single symbol, or a single letter. Trademarks are a product identifier.

- **Service Identifiers** — A word, phrase, design, logo, or shape that uniquely identifies a business unit in a particular service category, such as a restaurant or dealership.

- **Company Identifiers** — The legal name and logo that identifies a company.

Trademarks fall into the class of product identifiers. When distinctive colors, shapes, and ornaments are attached to a product or its packaging, these characteristics may also serve as a product identifier. These types of identifiers are commonly referred to as trade dress, design marks, or configuration marks.

Trademark Search

To ensure that a trademark does not infringe upon the trademark name of an existing commercial identifier, a chosen mark should be properly researched for prior existence. A search for an existing commercial identifier includes searching the Internet, business databases, and legal databases.

Before spending time and resources building up one's business or product, one should know whether the name chosen for that business or product can be used. There are search firms that for several hundred dollars can provide comprehensive data regarding companies and products using any given name. To acquire the data on whether a certain mark is already being used need not involve an attorney, but an attorney can analyze the data.

Establishing an Identifier

A trademark must exhibit a certain level of distinctiveness to be effective in uniquely identifying a product or service. The distinctiveness of the chosen mark must make consideration for whether it is generic, descriptive, suggestive, or arbitrary. The mark should not be capable of being confused with another similar product or trademark.

Registering a Trademark

Trademarks must be registered with the PTO, and in some instances one or more state trademark registries. A trademark should identify a product or service rather than a company. However, careful choice and design of a company identifier may allow the company identifier (or some part of it) to serve as a trademark also.

Trademarks vs. Patent Protection

Trademarks are used to protect the brand of a product by providing brand name recognition, while patents are used to protect the functional features of a product. However, patents have a limited term whereas trademarks remain attached to a product for the life of the product or for as long as the mark continues to be used for the product. Trademarks are also used to protect inventions that are not patentable. Inventions must meet certain requirements (as discussed in Chapter 1, *Requirements for a Patent*) to be patented. When an invention does not meet the requirements for a patent, a trademark may provide sufficient protection to monopolize the invention in the marketplace.

Using the Trademark

Unlike a patent, trademarks do not require maintenance fees to be paid after the mark is registered. A trademark, by default, is canceled if after the fifth year of registration, the trademark owner fails to file Section 8 Affidavit, which indicates that the mark is still in use. The cancellation takes place in the sixth year. After five years of registration, if no one challenges the mark and no court has ruled against ownership of the mark, the owner must file a Section 15 Affidavit before the end of the sixth year to complete trademark registration requirements. A Section 15 Affidavit must indicate that the mark has been in continuous use for the previous five years, continues to be used in commerce, and has not been subjected to any adverse court rulings.

chapter seven

Establishing Trade Secrets

Trade secrets have no filing requirements. Trade secrets are sensitive business information that gives a company the competitive edge. Any information, design, process, composition, technique, formula or device that is not generally known may be considered a trade secret. The establishment of trade secrets requires the establishment of a trade secret protection policy. It is in the best interest of a company to implement processes to prevent the disclosure of trade secret information to the general public. Businesses and owners of trade secrets must take reasonable precautions to keep their trade secrets confidential to acquire and maintain trade secret rights.

Trade Secret Protection Policy

All employees, consultants, advisors, contractors, suppliers, and any other contacts who have access to sensitive business information must adhere to the confidentiality established by a company's trade secrets. These employees and contacts must sign a confidentiality agreement, which binds them to the company's trade secret protection policy. Courts will enforce the terms of any reasonably drafted and implemented trade secret protection policy. The court may issue restraining orders or injunctions against a breaching party or anyone who collaborates with a breaching party in an effort to benefit from the breach. The courts may also award monetary damages to the exploited company.

Confidentiality Agreement

By signing a confidentiality agreement, the signed parties become responsible for any breach of the agreement. A breach of a confidentiality agreement is considered legal gross negligence or a breach of duty.

Trade Secrets vs. Patents

Trade secrets protect an invention after it is put into commercial use. If a patent application is filed within one year after an invention is put into commercial use, trade secret laws may protect the invention. If a one year elapses since the invention was first put into commercial use, any acquired patent will be ruled invalid. One of the requirements of patent laws is that the patent application must explain how to make and use an invention. As such, knowledge of the invention that may be protected by trade secret confidentiality is exposed to the public once a patent is published or acquired.

A trade secret offers perpetual protection that lasts forever or until the secret is discovered. Trade secrets offer the following advantages over patents.

- Trade secrets may be maintained without the cost and time required for completing the patent application process.

- Trade secrets do not require public disclosure, as do patents. As such, the design of the invention is not disclosed and made vulnerable to reverse engineering techniques.

- Trade secrets do not require the complexities of defining and assigning ownership or naming inventors.

- Trade secrets do not have to meet the requirements of novelty and usefulness that are required for patents.

- Trades secrets don't require government approval for their creation.

- Trade secrets may be used to protect minor details, changes, and new techniques that would require making application for additional patents.

- Trade secrets rights are immediate upon signing of a confidentiality agreement.

Though trade secrets offer many advantages over patents, there are some disadvantages of using trade secrets alone as a means of protection. If a trade secret is discovered, despite attempts to keep sensitive company information confidential, the trade secret is lost forever. Though patents allow for the public disclosure of an invention, a patent also protects against any infringement. If an outside party develops an invention and patents it using trade secrets of an unpatented invention, the original inventor has no recourse in preventing the establishment of the patent. Even worse, the new inventor, through the establishment of the patent, may sue the original inventor for patent infringement. The original inventor must then be able to prove that his use of the invention preceded the patent application by more than one year.

chapter eight

Establishing Patent Ownership

A patent provides an inventor with the exclusive right to make, use, sell, or import an invention for a fixed period of time. The PTO issues three types of patents- utility, design, and plant patents. A patent must be supported by claims that show the invention meets the technological requirements established for each particular type of patent.

Only the inventor is allowed to apply for a patent. Under certain circumstances, another party may make application on behalf of the inventor. Such circumstances include the following:

- The inventor is deceased. The administrator or executor of the inventor's estate may make application.

- The inventor is mentally incompetent. A guardian may make application.

- The inventor refuses to apply. A joint inventor or other person having proprietary interest in the invention may apply.

- The inventor cannot be found. A joint inventor or other person having proprietary interest in the invention may apply.

If a person other than the inventor or other than those persons indicated above should make application for an invention, any issued patent would be invalid. If a person falsely identifies himself or herself as an inventor, that person may be subject to criminal prosecution. Personnel of the PTO are also prohibited from applying for a patent or otherwise acquiring patent rights unless the patent or patent right is acquired through bequest or inheritance.

Patent ownership is a contentious issue since the owner of a patent is the party who is entitled to control the manufacture and sale of the patented invention. Issues of patent ownership are an extension of invention ownership issues. If the invention had multiple contributors or was created under an employer-employee relationship, ownership issues may be resolved with the use of an agreement. In more complex situations, professional assistance may be necessary to establish ownership.

Every application for a patent must include a signature of both the inventor and the potential patent owner. If a patent application fails to list all contributing inventors, patent rights will be loss if it can be proved that the error was made in bad faith. If an error is not made in bad faith, the mistake may be corrected with no loss of patent rights.

The Inventor as Owner

An inventor is the person who creates the novelty of an invention. An inventor develops concepts that make an invention novel and non-obvious. Novelty and non-obviousness are the basis for the claims that must be presented to obtain a patent. Often the inventor retains ownership of a patented invention and licenses or sells patent rights to others. A license provides another party with permission to make use of or sell the invention for a limited time period in return for making royalty payments to the patent owner. The inventor may also manufacture and sell an invention to maintain monopoly rights over the patent, or the inventor may transfer full or partial patent rights to another party through an assignment. Patent right assignments are usually exchanged for money, but patent rights may be assigned in exchange for other things as specified by the terms of an assignment agreement.

Joint Inventors as Owners

When more than one person is responsible for developing a patentable invention, the joint owners are required to sign the patent application as both inventors and owners. An inventor is anyone who contributes to an inventive concept that becomes part of at least one patent. Joint inventors are two or more parties who make such a contribution. Joint ownership of an invention is not dependent upon whether the parties physically work together or work together at the same time, nor is it dependent upon the amount of contribution made to the invention. A joint owner need only make a contribution.

A party who participates in an invention process by building or testing the invention is not considered to be an inventor. An inventor must contribute to the inventive concept, which means an inventor must have made a contribution of at least one novel and non-obvious concept that qualifies the invention for patentability. If in building or testing the invention, a second party develops a novel and non-obvious method that improves the invention, the second party may then be considered an inventor.

Issues of ownership often result in disputes between inventors. However, it is commonplace for joint inventors to decide ownership issues among themselves, such as how to divide revenue and profits by engaging a contractual joint ownership agreement. In the absence of such an agreement, issues of joint ownership may be resolved by an examination of events recorded in lab notebooks. Other inventions are developed with the use of a Consultant's Agreement in which contributors to an invention agree to assign all patent rights to a particular inventor. Without either of these documents, a dispute can be quite lengthy and expensive, as mediators or the courts will have to intervene. Courts have a final say on ownership issues that are presented before them.

The PTO has established special rules regarding joint patent ownership and the division of income from patents. PTO rules specify the following:

- Joint inventors are required to consent to an assignment of all rights to the patent.

- Unless otherwise specified by an agreement, any joint owner may make, sell, or use the invention without consent from other owners and without paying compensation to other owners.

These rules do not require that joint owners share equally in the exploitation of a patent. The rules allow for joint owners to compete against one another in the marketing and selling of the joint invention. The owners must enter into a joint ownership agreement to ensure that proceeds are fairly distributed and to protect their interests in an invention.

Joint Ownership Agreements

Joint ownership issues may include commercial exploitation, financial shares, accounting practices, and inequities among competing inventors. All of these issues are easily resolved with use of Joint Owner's Agreement (JOA) which should include the following:

- Language that prevents any one joint owner from exploiting the patent without consent from the other joint owners, except in the case of a dissenter. In such a situation, a majority vote may overrule a dissenter's actions.

- Methods for resolving disputes usually involve engaging

the services of an arbitrator when the joint owners are not capable of reaching dispute resolution.

- Language that provides for all joint owners to share profits in proportion to their interest in expenditures and income. Generally, when one joint owner disagrees with expenditure, the other joint owners will advance the amount necessary for the expenditure and then collect an increased return from any income produced, usually double the cost of the expenditure.

- Language that dictates if a joint owner chooses to manufacture or sell the invention, that owner must pay royalties to all other joint owners as well as the manufacturing owner.

The Employer as Owner

In most instances, when an inventor is employed and develops an invention while employed, the inventor is obligated to transfer rights for the invention to the employer. The employer may acquire rights in one of three ways as follows:

1. A contractual Employment Agreement.
2. "Employed to Invent" Rules.
3. Shop Rights.

Employment Agreement

An employment agreement requires that employees sign an agreement, as part of their employment, which includes provisions that allow for the employee to relinquish ownership rights in advance of creating any invention. This type of employment agreement is also termed, pre-invention assignment. The agreement specifies the circumstances under which the employer owns an invention created by an employee. The employee is obligated to assign ownership to the employer for any inventions developed under the following circumstances:

- The invention is developed during the term of employment.

- The employer relates the invention to the employer's existing business practices or any business practices contemplated.

- The invention is developed on the employer's clock, in other words, during the employee's paid work hours.

- The invention is developed using the employer's time, facilities, or resources.

- The invention is developed within the scope of the employee's duties.

When an employee develops an invention away from the workplace, on his own time, using his own resources, the inventor may still be obligated to assign ownership to his or her employer. The obligation of an employee to assign an invention to his or her employer when the invention falls within the scope of the employee's duties and the obligation to assign an invention that is related to business practices contemplated by the employer provides the employer with broad coverage for ownership. Employers may also require that employed inventors disclose any inventions developed, no matter where and how the invention was developed, so that the employer may determine if the invention is assignable to him or herself.

Eight states impose restrictions on the assignment of inventions created by inventor-employees. The states of California, Delaware, Illinois, Kansas, Minnesota, North Carolina, Utah, and Washington impose such restrictions. The restrictions dictate that an employee cannot be required to assign rights for an invention that the employee developed entirely on his or her own time, without the use of the employer's resources unless

- The invention is related to the employer's business or research and development (R&D) at the time of conception or when the invention was reduced to practice.

- The invention resulted from work performed by the employee, for the employer.

An employer's resources include equipment, supplies, facilities, and trade secrets. An employer's research and development is inclusive of actual R&D as well as demonstrably anticipated R&D.

The states of California, Illinois, Kansas, Minnesota, and Washington further require that inventor-employees be provided with a written notice of such restrictions. In these states, if employees are not provided such notice, employer assignments are not enforceable. In those states that impose restrictions but do not require notice, state laws exist to prevent employers from requiring assignments that are considered grossly unfair.

When an employer requires that employee-inventors disclose all inventions developed, the terms of the employment agreement as well as the laws of the state in which the employer is located establish the right of ownership. If the employer is satisfied that he or she is not entitled to ownership of a disclosed invention, the employee must apply for a release of the invention. A release is a document that reassigns or returns an invention to the employer from the employee. Under certain conditions, the employer may retain a shop right to the released invention. A shop right, as discussed below, gives an employer a right to use (not own) the invention for personal or business purposes.

If an employee disregards the terms of an employment agreement or attempts to license an invention in violation of the terms specified in the employment agreement, the employer may sue the employee for breach of contract. If an employee is found guilty of such a breach, the employee may become liable to pay monetary damages to the employer and also assign ownership of the invention to the employer.

Employed to Invent

When an employee is employed to invent, the employer specifically hires the employee for the purpose of developing inventions. This type of hiring principle is also termed, "hired to invent." The employer is not required to draft a written agreement to define the ownership of inventions since it is already implied by the nature of the employment. A 1952 Supreme Court ruling specifically addressed the issue as follows, "One employed to make an invention, who succeeds during his term of service in accomplishing the task, is bound to assign to his employer any patent obtained." Despite the ruling, many employers prefer to use an employment agreement because the agreement is more easily enforced than rights implied by the Supreme Court's ruling.

Shop Right

A shop right is a right incurred by an employer under special circumstances to make use of an invention created by an employee. There are a number of circumstances that may lead to shop right, but most notable are when the employee uses the employer's resources to create an invention or creates an invention on the employer's clock. A shop right differs from the rights implied by an employment agreement or the employed-to-invent rule. A shop right does not provide the employer with right of ownership for an invention. A shop right provides an employer with a limited right to use the invention, not a right to own the invention. Shop rights are derived from state laws and court rulings. The employer generally uses shop right as a defense when an employee patents an invention and sues the employer for infringing upon the patent. As an example, an employee is hired as a service technician for a utility company. The service technician finds fault in a device that he is required to install. He conceives a device that corrects the fault and the employer uses the device for all future installations. The service technician later patents the device that corrects the fault. The service technician is not bound by an invention agreement and he was not hired as an inventor. However, the service technician made use of the employer's resources while employed as a service technician for the employer. The service technician sues the employer for infringement because of the employer's use of the invention. The employer is entitled to shop right for the use of his resources in developing the invention. When an employer acquires limited use rights under the shop right principle, the employee-inventor retains ownership of the invention and the employer may use the invention without having to pay the employee-inventor for that use.

Employer Patents

In the United States an inventor must be named as the applicant for a patent application even if the inventor assigns ownership to another party. If the inventor is obligated to assign an invention to his or her employer under an invention agreement, the employee is required to sign a formal assignment of patent rights and file the assignment with the PTO. The employer is listed as an assignee while the employee is listed as the inventor.

To encourage inventor-employees to continue to invent and to submit disclosures of new inventions, employers may offer employees incentives such as the following:

- Salary increases.
- Monetary bonuses for each signing of a company patent application.
- A share of royalties generated by the invention.
- Partial ownership of a subsidiary entity.

Acquiring Joint Ownership

An individual need not be an inventor to acquire joint patent ownership. Joint patent ownership may be acquired by assignment for money, assignment to a partnership, or created by a will. In return for money or some other mutually agreed upon compensation, a patent owner may assign a portion of his or her interest in a patent since patent rights are a form of personal property. In the case of death of a patent owner, patent rights are willed to the heirs or beneficiaries of the deceased patent owner just as with any other form of personal property.

Many patent owners choose to perfect and improve their inventions, but they don't always have the means to do so. One way for patent owners to obtain assistance in improving or perfecting an invention is to assign a portion of patent ownership to a partnership, which is capable of providing the necessary expertise or funds to advance the patented invention.

Assigning Patent Ownership

A patent is personal property and like other forms of personal property, a patent may be sold, mortgaged, bequeathed, or inherited. Patent laws also dictate that patents or an application for a patent may be transferred or sold by a legal instrument provided in writing. This legal instrument is termed, an assignment. An assignment may be used to transfer the interest in patent in part or in whole. The person in receipt of the assigned patent becomes the owner and is entitled to the same rights as the original patent owner. The PTO, in the grant of a patent, does not usually specify the terms of an assignment. However, in some parts of the United States, the PTO may grant a patent with the same character of interest that is afforded by an assignment. An assignment must be acknowledged and witnessed by a notary public or an officer who is authorized to perform notary acts or administer oaths.

A mortgaged patent property passes ownership to the Mortgage Company or lender until the terms of the mortgage are satisfied.

A conditional assignment also passes ownership in the same manner and is considered absolute until the involved parties or a decree of a competent court cancels it.

The PTO records all assignments, grants, and other instruments received for recording. The recording of relative instruments serves as notice of the particular instrument. If a patent grant, patent assignment, conveyance of a patent, or interest in either a patent or patent application is not recorded within three months from its date of signatures, such instruments become void, without notice, against any subsequent purchaser. The only exception is if the recording was accomplished prior to the sale.

If a patent application is assigned and the assignment is recorded on or before the date on which the issue fee is paid, the patent will be issued to the assignee. If the assignment is for partial interest in the patent, the patent will be issued to the joint owners - the inventor and the assignee.

Professional Assistance

Because of the complexity in establishing a patent, the inventor will need some professional assistance at some time during the process. Patents are governed by IP laws, which are legal procedures that are often characterized by any number of nuances, loopholes, and exceptions. The establishment of a patent also has international implications that may be more easily addressed by a professional. The volume of both national and international patent issues has caused many changes and modifications to patent and IP laws.

The PTO establishes rules and regulations governing the conduct and practices of professional patent agents and patent attorneys. The PTO accredits, licenses, and registers such professionals. Registered and licensed patent agents and attorneys must have demonstrated to the PTO that they have the legal, scientific, and technical skills as well as the moral character and reputation to be able to assist patent applicants. Accredited patent attorneys and agents are authorized by the PTO to prepare and prosecute patent applications on behalf of the inventor. They may offer opinions on patentability, but only licensed patent attorneys are entitled to extend their services to representing an inventor in court matters. The complexity of IP laws and issues has led many practicing professionals to narrow their practice to specific areas of the field. If an inventor is having issues with a design patent, he or she may find it more advantageous to seek a patent professional who specializes in design patents.

By engaging the services of a licensed patent professional, an inventor must appoint the chosen patent attorney with power of attorney or appoint the chosen patent agent with authorization of agent. Appropriate forms must be completed and filed with the PTO to document the appointment. Once a patent attorney or patent agent has been documented as appointed to handle the patenting of an invention, the PTO will direct all correspondence to the appointed professional, not the inventor or applicant. The PTO will only communicate with the inventor on issues regarding the status of a patent application. An inventor may relinquish and revoke the appointment of a patent agent or attorney at any time.

In the same manner that the PTO licenses and registers patent agents and attorneys, the PTO also has the power to disbar or suspend such professionals from practicing. The PTO will accept and act upon complaints of misconduct or other wrongdoings by patent attorneys and agents. The PTO will make a decision as to the legitimacy of the behavior or act after conducting a hearing and receiving evidence of the wrongdoing. In general, disputes over the fees charged for services are not the basis for disbarment or suspension. However, a complaint that identifies a case of gross overcharging may be considered for such actions.

chapter nine

The Patent Search

In order to be patented, an invention must meet very specific requirements to include requirements that indicate the invention is new and innovative. To ensure that a newly submitted patent application does not infringe upon an invention that has already been patented, a patent search is required for all patents. A patent search is a time consuming and costly endeavor; however, it is a necessary one. There are several types of patent searches that may be explored.

- **Bibliographic search.** Bibliographic searches are patent searches for the purpose of locating specific items, such as all patents owned by an employee or patents that may include prior-art. Bibliographic searches are commonplace for inventors as well as attorneys and businesses specifically involved in the patenting of inventions.

- **Anticipation (or patentability) search.** Anticipation searches are patent searches for the purpose of determining whether an invention is likely to qualify for a patent. This type of patent search is more complex than a bibliographic search because it requires the searcher to analyze current patents, expired patents, and other related prior-art to assist in determining the novelty and non-obviousness of an invention. A positive result from an anticipation search is a result that indicates the invention is most likely to meet the requirements to be patentable. As such, a positive result provides the inventor with assurance in moving forward with efforts to develop, market, license or sell the invention.

- **Infringement search.** An infringement search is made when one party sues another party for patent infringement. This type of search is even more complex than an anticipation search because the infringing party must convince a court that the PTO made a mistake in issuing a patent to the patent holder. In other words, the infringing party attempts to prove the existing patent invalid.

- **State-of-the-art search.**

- **Patent title search.**

The simpler forms of patent searches may be performed over the Internet. More complex searches must be performed by searching either Patent and Trademark Depository Libraries (PTDLs), patents stored at the PTO, or engaging the services of a professional patent searcher.

Searching the PTO

The PTO publishes all U.S. patents and their accompanying drawings on the day they are issued. The PTO is located in Virginia and stores hardcopy or microfiche copies of more than 6,000,000 issued patents, arranged by classification.

The PTO also stores the following material using the same classifications that are used for patents:

- Foreign patents.

- Patent assignments.

- Examiner's search files.

- Literature.

- Reference materials.

Literature and reference materials include documents such as dictionaries, manuals, indices, and the Official Gazette.

The Official Gazette is the PTO's official journal relating to patents and trademarks. The journal is published as a weekly online publication, which announces all patents being issued and trademarks being registered or published for opposition. The publication is issued in two parts, one part describing patents and the other part describing trademarks. The publication provides the following information for each listed patent.

- Patent application serial number.

- Patent number.

- U.S. classification.

- International classification.

- Inventor's name and address.

- Assignees.

- Filing date.

- Number of claims.

- Sample claim or abstract.

In addition, the Official Gazette includes a selected figure taken from the drawings provided with issued patents. Patent illustrations and claims are listed in order of subject matter classification to permit access to issued patents in a given technology. The publication contains other useful patent information, such as notices of patent and trademark lawsuits, patents available for license, patents available for sale, an index of patents and patent owners, a list of PTDLs, court orders, notices, changes in classification, and rule changes. Copies of the Official

Gazette are also available at PTDLs and public libraries.

Printed copies of patents may be purchased from the PTO at cost. The patent number must be used to identify the requested patent. The PTO also provides a "Patent Search Room" that is open for public use in the search and examination of patents. The Patent Search Room makes U.S. patents issued since 1790 available to the public without cost. Like with most library systems, staff is available to assist the public with locating information. The PTO has different locations for patent search information. The Public Patent Search and Image Retrieval Facility (PSIRF) is often referred to as the public search room. Most searchers make use of this facility. A Files Information Room contains records and files associated with issued patents. The examining division of the PTO maintains examiner's search files at a location that is more secure than the public search room. Visitors must make application and obtain permission to search the examiner's search files. The Scientific and Technical Information Center is available for public use. The center houses about 90,000 volumes of bound technical and scientific periodicals and more than 120,000 volumes of technical and scientific books, written in various languages. The center also stores the official journals of 77 foreign patent organizations and 40,000,000 foreign patents are available in either paper form or electronically stored on microfilm, microfiche or CD-ROM.

The PTO also provides the capability to perform electronic patent searches through its EAST and WEST terminal servers. The WEST terminal provides a web-based access system that may be accessed by Internet users and PTDL searchers. The EAST terminal may be accessed at the PTO and certain PTDLs. The EAST terminal may be used to perform Boolean and keyword searches indexed on classes and sub-classes. The system is configured to perform both forward and backward patent searches. In other words, the computer system will allow users to search backward in time and forward in time for prior-art or patents. The EAST terminal server may be used to search U.S., Japanese, and European patents for free, but the PTO charges a fee to print from the system.

Searching PTDLs

PTDLs may be found in most major cities. A search of PTDL resources provides for a less thorough search than is available from a search of resources at the PTO. PTDLs may not have all U.S. patents and are not likely to have foreign patents, other non-patent literature, or reference materials available. PTDLs do not provide data sufficient to perform a true search. The most useful data are stored on the periodically published CASSIS/CLASS and CASSIS/BIB CD-ROMs. Each PTDL subscribes to the PTO for its periodically released patent data. The data contains only classifications and bibliographic information; it does include patents stored by subject or classification. CASSIS/CLASS may be used to obtain classification information for any patent or the list of patents in each classification issued from 1790 to the present. CASSIS/BIB CD may be used to locate the following information:

- The classification of any recently issued patent.

- All patents assigned to a particular company or a particular individual.

- Listing of patents by year of issuance.

- The status of all patents applied using a particular residence.

- Recently issued patents with certain words or phrases in the title or abstract.

- The field of search for a type of invention.

Most PTDLs provide searchers with access to the PTO's WEST

terminal server. A select few PTDLs provide searchers with access to the EAST terminal server. Access is usually provided at an hourly rate that is established by the particular PTDL. PTDLs located in the 50 United States as well U.S. possessions and territories are shown at Table 2.

State Patent and Trademark Depository Libraries

State	Patent and Trademark Depository Libraries
Alabama	• Ralph Brown Draughon Library, Auburn University
	• Birmingham Public Library
Alaska	• Z.J. Loussac Public Library
	• Anchorage Municipal Libraries
Arizona	• Noble Science & Engineering Library, Arizona State University
Arkansas	• Arkansas State Library – Little Rock
California	• Los Angeles Public Library
	• California State Library – Sacramento
	• San Diego Public Library
	• San Francisco Public Library
	• Sunnyvale Center for Innovation, Inventions, and Ideas
Colorado	• Denver Public Library
Delaware	• University of Delaware Library – Newark
District of Columbia	• Founders Library, Howard University
Florida	• Broward County Main Library – Fort Lauderdale
	• Miami-Dade Public Library
	• University of Central Florida Libraries – Orlando
	• Tampa Campus Library, University of South Florida
Georgia	• Library and Information Center, Georgia Institute of Technology – Atlanta
Hawaii	• Hawaii State Library – Honolulu
Idaho	• University of Idaho Library – Moscow
Illinois	• Chicago Public Library
	• Illinois State University – Springfield

State Patent and Trademark Depository Libraries	
State	Patent and Trademark Depository Libraries
Indiana	• Marion County Public Library – Indianapolis
	• Siegesmund Engineering Library, Purdue University – West Lafayette
Iowa	• State Library of Iowa – Des Moines
Kansas	• Ablah Library, Wichita State University – Wichita
Kentucky	• Louisville Free Public Library
Louisiana	• Troy H. Middleton Library, Louisiana State University – Baton Rouge
Maine	• Raymond H. Fogler Library, University of Maine – Orono
Maryland	• Engineering & Physical Sciences Library, University of Maryland – College Park
Massachusetts	• Physical Sciences & Engineering Library, University of Massachusetts - Amherst
	• Boston Public Library
Michigan	• Media Union Library, University of Michigan – Ann Arbor
	• Abigail S. Timme Library, Ferris State University– Big Rapids
	• Great lakes Patent and Trademark Center, Detroit public Library – Detroit
Minnesota	• Minneapolis Public Library and Information Center
Mississippi	• Mississippi Library Commission – Jackson
Missouri	• Linda Hall Library – Kansas City
	• St. Louis Public Library
Montana	• University of Montana Library – Butte
Nebraska	• Engineering Library, University of Nebraska-Lincoln – Lincoln
Nevada	• University Library, University of Nevada-Reno – Reno
New Hampshire	• New Hampshire State Library – Concord
New Jersey	• Newark Public Library
	• Library of Science & Medicine, Rutgers University – Piscataway
New Mexico	• Centennial Science & Engineering Library, The University of New Mexico – Albuquerque

Table 2 - State Patent and Trademark Depository Libraries

State Patent and Trademark Depository Libraries	
State	Patent and Trademark Depository Libraries
New York	• New York State Library – Albany
	• Buffalo and Erie County Public Library
	• Science, Industry and Business Library, New York Public Library
North Carolina	• D.H. Hill Library, North Carolina State University – Raleigh
North Dakota	• Chester Fritz Library, University of North Dakota – Grand Forks
Ohio	• Summit County Public Library – Akron
	• Public Library of Cincinnati and Hamilton County - Cincinnati
	• Cleveland Public Library
	• Ohio State University Libraries – Columbus
	• Toledo and Lucas County Public Library
Oklahoma	• Oklahoma State University – Still water
Oregon	• Lewis and Clark College – Portland
Pennsylvania	• The Free Library of Philadelphia
	• The Carnegie Library of Pittsburgh
	• Pattee Library, Pennsylvania State University – University Park
Puerto Rico	• General Library, University of Puerto Rico – Mayagüez
Rhode Island	• Providence Public library
South Carolina	• R. M. Cooper Library, Clemson University
South Dakota	• Devereaux Library, South Dakota School of Mines and Technology – Rapid City
Tennessee	• Memphis and Shelby County Public Library and Information Center
	• Stevenson Science and Engineering Library, Vanderbilt University – Nashville
Texas	• McKinney Engineering Library, University of Texas at Austin
	• Sterling C. Evans Library, Texas A&M University – College Station
	• Dallas Public Library
	• Fondren Library, Rice University – Houston
	• Texas Tech University Library – Lubbock

State Patent and Trademark Depository Libraries	
State	Patent and Trademark Depository Libraries
Utah	• Marriot Library, University of Utah – Salt Lake City
Vermont	• Bailey Howe Library, University of Vermont – Burlington
Virginia	• James Branch Cabell Library, Virginia Commonwealth University – Richmond
Washington	• Engineering Library, University of Washington – Seattle
West Virginia	• Evansdale Library, West Virginia University – Morgantown
Wisconsin	• Kurt F. Wendt Library, University of Wisconsin-Madison – Madison
	• Milwaukee Public Library
Wyoming	• Natrona County Public Library – Casper

Table 2 - State Patent and Trademark Depository Libraries

Searching the Internet

A computer search of patents provides a good source of preliminary information to be used in a patent search, but the information provided is not sufficient for determining the patentability or validity of a patent. However, computer searches are provided at minimal costs and are relatively easy to use. Computer search databases are usually limited to patents issued as of 1971 or 1976 and will not be capable of providing information on prior-art established before such dates.

Several different databases are available for online searches. They include a free database provided by the PTO on its Web site at **www.uspto.gov**. The PTO database provides access to a text searchable database of patents and patent drawings issued as of January 1976. The Web site presents patent drawings as images that are stored using G4 compression TIFF format. A link to a downloadable TIFF viewer is provided for users that do not have the capability to display such images.

The following fee-based databases are also accessible over the

Internet:

Delphion

The Delphion Web site, located at **www.delphion.com**, is an extension of the former IBM patent Web site. The Web site may be used to search patents issued as of 1971. Upgrades to the Delphion site are expected to include pre 1971 patents, European Patent Office patents, collections from the World Intellectual Property Organization and abstracts from the Derwent World Patent Index (DWPI). Forty international patent issuing authorities provide input to the DWPI.

Micropatent

The Micropatent Web site, located at **www.micropatent.com**, may be used to search U.S. and Japanese patents issued as of 1976. The site provides methods of searching International PCT patents issued as of 1983 and European patents issued as of 1988. The Micropatent Web site also provides access to the Official Gazette for patents.

LexPat

The LexPat Web site, located at **www.lexis-nexis.com**, may be used to search U.S. patents issued as of 1971. The site also provides access to an extensive library of technical journals and magazines that be used to research prior-art.

QPAT

The QPAT Web site, located at **www.qpat.com**, may be used to search U.S. patents issued as of 1974.

PatentMax

The PatentMax Web site, located at **www.patentmax.com**, may be used to search U.S. and foreign patents.

IP Search Engine

The IP Search Engine, located at **www.IPSearchEngine.com**, may be used to search numerous databases using "concept" searching, which is a more complete search technique than that offered by Boolean searching.

PatBase

The PatBase Web site, located at **www.patbase.com**, may be used to search patents that date back to the 1800s. The site provides access to patent data held by numerous nations.

Professional Patent Searchers

The most thorough patent application requires that the applicant have knowledge of patent rules, patent laws, practices, and procedures used by the PTO and scientific or technical knowledge of the concepts, which underlie the particular invention. These types of skills and knowledge are best acquired from patent experts even though an unskilled person is not prohibited from making application. Though patents have been issued for patents applied by unskilled persons, those patents may not be effective in providing adequate protection of an invention. There are two types of professional patent searchers: licensed and unlicensed searchers. Licensed patent searchers include patent attorneys and patent agents who are licensed by the PTO. Patent searchers charge fees for their services. Fees may be assessed by the hour or they may charge a flat rate. Unlicensed searchers usually charge less for their services. Unlicensed searchers may charge fees in the range of $100 to $500. Licensed searchers, on the other hand, may charge fees in the range of $300 to $1,200. While the PTO cannot and will not make recommendation for a particular patent attorney or patent agent, the PTO does maintain a registry of patent professionals who are recognized by the PTO as having acquired and exhibited the necessary professionalism to assist in making application for a patent.

The PTO licenses patent agents to prepare and prosecute patent applications. Patent agents have technical training, typically, an undergraduate degree in engineering. They are authorized to perform patent searches and offer opinions on the patentability of an invention, but they are not attorneys. Patent agents may not appear in court or handle infringement lawsuits.

The PTO also licenses patent attorneys. In addition, patent attorneys must be licensed by at least one state authority, in at least one state. The most popular licensing authorities include the state bar and state Supreme Court. A general practice attorney that is licensed to practice law in one or more states, but is not licensed by the PTO is not authorized to prepare patent applications nor is he or she authorized to use the title "patent attorney."

Unlicensed searchers do not have expert credentials and are not authorized to provide opinions regarding patentability. Individuals and companies that advertise to perform patent related duties, such as patent searching and invention marketing, but are not registered with the PTO, cannot represent an invention owner before the PTO. The PTO does not recognize such individuals and organizations and will not assist inventors in dealing with such non-professionals.

Patent searches have limitations (discussed later) that prevent 100 percent accuracy in the search process. Professional patent searchers should be provided with as much information as necessary to perform as accurate a search as possible. Patent searchers may be provided inventor notebooks and invention disclosures as well as the following:

- Complete and thorough descriptions of the invention.

- All relevant drawings.

- Descriptions of all applicable novel features of the invention.

- Any deadlines associated with the invention or patent filing.

- A related patent that identifies the class of patents to be searched.

The information provided to patent searchers might contain confidential information that the inventor may use a trade secret. Patent agents and attorneys have a legal obligation to refrain from disclosing confidential information that may accompany information documenting the invention. Confidential communication laws bind these licensed professionals to secrecy. Unlicensed patent searchers, on the other hand, are not bound to the laws of confidential communication. Unlicensed patent searchers should be required to sign a confidentiality agreement to protect against their disclosing confidential information about an invention to outside parties. To guard against theft of information provided in submitted documents, inventors are encouraged to blank out any dates entered on the documents.

Patent searchers may be located by searching the following resources.

- The Internet and the PTO Web site at **www.upsto.gov**.

- Advertisements in periodicals, such as the Journal of the Patent and Trademark Office society, a publication of an association of patent examiners.

- The PTO publication, Attorneys and Agents Registered to Practice before the U.S. Patent and Trademark Office (A&ARTP).

- Patent and Trademark Depository Libraries.
- Government bookstores.

In general, a professional and licensed patent searcher, located in the Washington, D.C.-Virginia vicinity, should be sought if a search requires an examination of patents stored at the PTO. This eliminates the additional expense of having an attorney, or an assistant to the attorney travel to Virginia to search the PTO library of patents. Patent searchers located in the Washington, D.C.-Virginia area are listed in the PTO's A&ARTP publication under ZIP code 22202 in both the District of Columbia and Virginia sections of the publication.

Patent Searching Process

To perform a patent search, regardless of complexity of the search, the searcher needs to establish the appropriate terms to describe the invention and then determine the relevant classification of the invention. Patent and patent information are stored in electronic databases or manual library systems. Even when patents are stored in library systems, their location within a manual storage system is usually electronically indexed. Patents are arranged according to the U.S. Patent Classification System. The system is comprised of more than 400 classes and 136,000 sub-classes of patents. The public may access the listing of all U.S. patents, which are arranged in numerical order and similar numerical listings published in the Official Gazette. Professional patent searchers should be familiar with the terminology used by the PTO to index and classify patents. If a patent search is being performed without the services of a professional searcher, the inventor must become familiar with the terminology to perform an accurate search. One of the searching methodologies used for most electronic systems, including those used online, at the PTO and at the various depositories includes a system of Boolean logic. Boolean logic is mathematical reasoning based the values "TRUE" and "FALSE", using the logical operators "AND," "OR," and "NOT." As an example, patents are being searched for a light bulb invention. The indexing system would require a search of the terms "light" and "bulb." A Boolean search will result in the following outcome:

Logical Search Terms "light" AND "bulb"	
TRUE	If a patent exists
FALSE	If no patent exists

A Boolean result of "TRUE" causes the computer software to also reveal the location of the patent. A Boolean result of "FALSE" signifies that no patent exits and ends the logical search for the terms, light and bulb.

The PTO has also established a manual search system and patent number search system that may be used to search patents using its online Web site. A manual search system allows the user to enter command line syntax to search patents. Command line syntax is computer instruction that is unique to a particular computer system. The syntax instructs the computer to behave in accordance with the instruction.

The patent searcher must also be familiar with the PTO's system of classifying inventions. Each invention class and subclass is given a unique number index. The classifications and their index values are published in a number of references including the following:

- **Index to the U.S. Patent Classification.**

    o   Alphabetical listing of all possible subject areas with classes and subclasses defined for each.

    o   Alphabetical listing of classes.

- **Manual of Classification.**

    o Numerical listing of classes with subclass listings under each.

- **Classification Definitions.**

    o Defines every class and subclass contained in the Manual of Classification.

    o Cross-references every subclass to additional references that correspond to the particular subclass.

Each of these references is available either over the Internet, in hard copy, or on electronic mediums, such as CD-ROM.

Patent Search Limitations

Even when the most complex search is made with the most skilled searcher, limitations in the search process ensure that no patent search results are accurate. Limitations include the following:

- There is no way to search pending and unpublished patent applications.

- Hard copy patents may not include all prior-art references.

- The search library or database may not include foreign, non-patent, or exotic references.

- The most recently issued patents may not yet be included in patent libraries or patent databases.

- Patents may be improperly classified and stored.

- An invention may have been publicly used but not published.

- An invention may have been previously invented but not published.

Patent Search Results

A completed patent search should include a list of relevant classes and subclasses included in the search, patent examiners consulted for the search and a listing of relevant patents and references discovered, with a brief discussion of each. Actual copies of references should accompany the listing of references. References may include U.S. patents, foreign patents, magazine articles and other published documents as indicated in the listing. If a licensed patent searcher conducts the search, this professional is authorized to render an opinion as to the patentability of an invention. Such an opinion may be provided for an additional $200 to $400 fee.

If the invention is a relatively simple device, composition, or process, the question of patentability is usually yes or no. More complex inventions will receive a more detailed opinion. The inventor not only needs to patent an invention, but also needs to have the patent provide meaningful and broad coverage. The scope of patent coverage is determined by the novelty and non-obviousness of the invention. An inventor needs broad enough coverage that competitors are not able to produce a competitive device easily or reproduce a process that is functionally equivalent to the patented device, yet not infringe on the patented device. The fewer non-obvious novel features that distinguish an invention over prior-art, the broader the patent coverage. If many non-obvious novel features are required to distinguish the invention from prior-art, the range of coverage is narrowed and an infringer has a better chance of producing a device or creating a process that would achieve the same results without infringing on the patent.

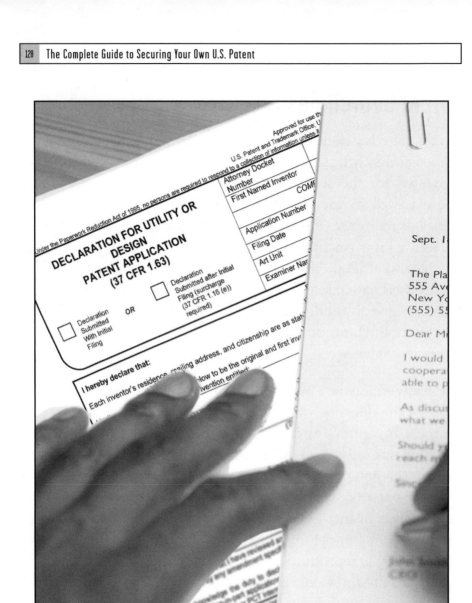

chapter ten

Filing a Patent Application

An inventor must file and sign an application for a U.S. patent even if the inventor does not have ownership of the invention. Some foreign patent applications, on the other hand, may be filed and signed by either the inventor or owner of the invention. If the inventor is incapacitated or deceased at the time of filing, a legal representative may file and sign the application. The representative is required to document proof of his or her authority.

The PTO provides two types of filing applications for a patent, a provisional application and a non-provisional application. A provisional application provides a method of disclosing the invention and establishing an early priority date without the cost of filing a non-provisional application.

Provisional Patent Application (PPA)

Provisional patent applications (PPA) were established in 1995 to allow inventors to document the reduction to practice of an invention, provided that a non-provisional patent application would be filed within one year of filing the PPA. The one exception is that a PPA cannot be filed for a design patent. The PPA filing date may be used in determining whether a reference constitutes a prior-art or in determining who is entitled to a patent in a case of interference. A PPA serves as a substitute for documenting the development of an invention using a lab notebook. However, a PPA does not require witness signatures, as do entries in a lab notebook. Also, a PPA serves as an interim document for establishing reduction to practice while eliminating the expense of actually building and testing an invention. A PPA must contain the following components:

- A description of the invention that clearly explains how to make and use the invention.

- Drawings necessary to understand the description.

If there is more than one version or mode of an invention, the inventor is required to describe the best of all versions or modes of the invention. At the inventor's discretion, other components of a non-provisional patent application, such as claims, may be included with a PPA.

The cost to file a PPA is less than the cost required to file a non-provisional patent application. As of 2006, the cost of filing a PPA was $200 as compared to the $300 cost of filing a non-provisional utility patent application. Though the filing date of a PPA may be used to establish the pendency date for an invention, patent rights will extend for 20 years beyond the filing of the non-provisional patent application, which is required within one year after the PPA filing date.

By filing a PPA, an inventor may sell, publish, or show the invention without loss of U.S. patent rights. Anyone who attempts to file a patent application on the published invention would then have a later filing date than the inventor who published the invention. Thus, a PPA filing assures the applicant of first rights to the patent in a case of interference. However, if a non-provisional patent application is not filed within one-year of the PPA filing, the PPA is considered abandoned and the PPA filing date may no longer be used in deciding prior-art references or interference.

Should the invention change to the point that the description provided by the PPA is not sufficient to describe the invention, a new PPA would have to be filed for the "new" invention and the filing date would be that of the filing of the new PPA application.

The filing date of a provisional patent is the date on which the PTO receives a complete provisional application. Claims and declarations are not required for provisional applications. A complete provisional application must include the name of the inventor(s), a written description of the invention, appropriate drawings, applicable filing fees and a cover sheet, which clearly specifies that the application is a provisional application. A surcharge is applied if the filing fees or cover sheet are submitted at a date that is later than the date of the provisional application.

Non-Provisional Patent Applications

All non-provisional patent applications must be filed as written documents, inclusive of a specification and an oath or declaration. The specification includes a description of the invention and claims that define the scope of the invention. The application must also include drawings, when necessitated, and the appropriate filling fees. All documentation must be provided in English or in a verified translation of documents into English. Documents must be legibly typewritten or printed using dark permanent ink and portrait orientation on durable, non-glossy white paper. All pages of the document should be the same size, A4 or 8½ x 11 inches, with top and bottom margins of at least ¾ inch, a right margin of at least ¾ inch and a left margin of at least one inch. Page spacing should be either double-spaced or 1½ spacing. They should be consecutively numbered, with page numbers visibly centered either above or below the text, **starting** with page one. Document fonts and content should be sufficiently dark to be capable of reproduction.

A patent application is not considered complete until all required components of the application are complete and in compliance with established rules. Incomplete patent applications are not forwarded for examination. Instead, the PTO will notify the applicant of the deficiency and be given a time to bring the application within compliance. The PTO may include a surcharge for a new submission to an application. If the deficiencies are not corrected within the required time, the application will either be returned to the applicant or disposed of. The filling fee will be refunded to the applicant less a handling fee, as published in the PTO's schedule of fees.

The filing date of a non-provisional patent application will be documented as the date on which the PTO receives a complete and compliant application. All complete applications received at the PTO are numbered in serial order and the applicant is provided a filing receipt that indicates the serial number and filling date of the patent application. Applicants are advised to submit all components of an application as one complete application. If an incomplete application is supplemented by additional and requested components, each component must be signed by the applicant with a letter that clearly and accurately connects the additional components with the existing components of the application.

Patent laws require that all non-provisional patent applications include an oath or declaration. An oath declares that the inventor making application for a patent believes that he or she is truly the original or first inventor of the subject matter of the application. An oath commits the inventor to certain other allegations as required by law and/or the PTO. The oath must be sworn and signed before a notary public or other person designated to administer such oaths. A declaration may be used in lieu of an oath under certain circumstances as follows:

- When reissuing patents.
- When claiming matter originally described, but not originally claimed.
- When filing a divisional or continuing application.

A declaration does not need to be sworn before a notary public. The inventor or person authorized to file application for a patent on behalf of the inventor must sign either an oath or declaration, in person. The signature must include a full first, full last name, and middle initial or name, if applicable, for each inventor. A postal address and indication of citizenship are also required. The submitted oath or declaration will not be returned to the applicant under any circumstances. Copies of submitted documents may be photocopied and furnished to applicants for a fee.

Foreign Patents

The rights associated with U.S. patents do extend beyond the geographical borders of the United States. Patent infringement by parties of foreign nations is a complicated and expensive issue. To protect a patent against infringement from foreign nations, a U.S. patent owner must apply for patent rights in other nations. An act of infringement by a party of a foreign country may not justify filing application for a patent in that country if the expense of filing application, getting the patent, and the uncertainties of licensing and litigation are not justifiable. It is usually worthwhile to file patent applications in foreign countries if there is a significant market for the invention or if an inventor has acquired a foreign licensee for an invention. Otherwise, the high cost of acquiring foreign patent protection may far exceed the rate of return from the sale of the invention.

Almost all countries have specific patent laws. Some common laws that are found to be applicable to many foreign patents and foreign governments include the following:

- Publication of an invention before the date of application prevents the applicant from obtaining a patent.

- Maintenance fees are required.

- A patented invention must also be manufactured in the foreign country after a certain time has expired, usually three years. Failure to manufacture a patented invention in a foreign country may cause the patent to be voided in some countries while other countries require the granting of a compulsory license to applicants.

Countries that are not members of treaties that cover patent applications have some differences in their patent laws and practices. They may be substantially different from U.S. patent laws and procedures. Such differences include the following:

- **Opposition Proceedings.** In the United States if a patent application is examined and allowed, it is issued without further proceedings. Most foreign countries require that an opposition proceeding be held before actually issuing the patent. An opposition proceeding provides for the application to be published, and anyone in opposition to the patentability of the invention may submit prior art to the patent office in an effort to block the patent. While the United States has established that all patents applied as of November 29, 2000, be published for public viewing 18 months after the established filing date, no laws or procedures have been established to allow the public to oppose the patent.

- **Filing Application in the Name of an Assignee.** U.S. patent laws require that patents be applied for in the name of the inventor. However, in most foreign countries a patent may be applied for by an assignee. Some foreign countries may also require that the inventor be named in the application; others do not.

- **Lack of Novelty Examination.** Some small countries will not examine a patent application for novelty when application is filed directly with the particular patent office. When countries such as Portugal and Belgium are required to examine patent applications and those applications are not acquired through the EPO, these countries will issue the patent and rely upon the courts to determine novelty and non-obviousness if an infringement occurs.

- **Maintenance Fees during the Pendency Period.** Some countries, such as Netherlands, Germany, Italy, France, and the jurisdiction of the EPO, require that annual maintenance fees be paid for a patent application during its pendency period. If application is filed through the EPO, with the exception of Australia, no individual country fees are required until the Europatent issues and is registered in each particular country. However, annual EPO fees are required until the patent actually issues.

- **Lack of a Grace Period.** In most foreign countries, an inventor must get an effective filing date before any public release or sale of an invention. This may be accomplished by either filing in the foreign country or filing in the United States and then filing a corresponding application under the Paris Convention within one year. Most countries consider any public release of an invention in any country as prior art. Other countries only recognize the public release of an invention in their own country as prior art. Some countries allow for exhibitions at recognized trade shows as long as a patent application is filed within six months of the exhibition. U.S. patent laws allow for a one-year grace period between public disclosure and making application.

- **First to File Rather than First to Invent.** In the case of patent interference, most foreign countries will issue the patent to the first party to file application for the patent. This method is contrary to U.S. patent laws, which base the issuance of a patent on the first to invent rule. The first to file rule is more simple and economical to implement whereas the first to invent rule involves expensive, complicated litigation.

- **Difficulty with Japanese Patents.** Japan requires expensive filing, translation and examination fees. Patent examinations are not automatically initiated as a result of filing application. An examination must be requested separately and it takes about three years to complete. It is very difficult to get a patent allowed, but once it is allowed it is far less likely of being infringed or challenged. On the other hand, Japanese courts tend to interpret patents and patent claims narrowly, making it possible to make small variations to claims to avoid infringement.

U.S. Applicants for Foreign Patents

The rights of U.S. patents extend only to states, U.S. territories and possessions. If a U.S. inventor wants to patent an invention in a foreign nation, the inventor must apply for a patent in the particular nation of interest or in the regional patent office of the nation of interest. In most instances, a U.S. applicant receives a filing receipt from the PTO that permits the applicant to file for a patent in foreign countries. The permission is indicated on the filing receipt as "Foreign Filling License Granted 2006 July 10." Most inventors get this foreign filing license immediately. However, if the filing receipt fails to include such permission, the invention either has possible military applications or the inventor is barred from filing in foreign countries until six months after the U.S. filing date. In most instances, there is really no reason to file for a foreign patent before the six-month period following the U.S. filing date. The time delay provides the U.S. government with a chance to review the application for possible classification on the basis of national security. If the invention does prove to have military application, the inventor will fail to receive a foreign license and the PTO may also provide the inventor with a Secrecy Order that requires the inventor to keep the invention secret until the government declassifies it. Declassification usually takes about 12 years. Since a patent may not be issued until then, the government will compensate such inventors if the government makes use of the invention in the meantime. It is possible to file application for foreign patent that is under a Secrecy Order, but it very complex and requires the assistance of a patent attorney experienced with this type of situation.

U.S. patent owners may make use of reciprocal patent filing rules that are established by international agreements, also known as treaties. Treaties provide a method of establishing consistent treatment for inventors in nations that sign to become members of the treaty, known as signatory nations. The three most important treaties that affect U.S. patented inventions are the Paris Convention, the Patent Cooperation Treaty (PCT) and the European Patent Convention (EPC). The reciprocal treatment offered by signatory nations dictates that when an inventor from one signatory nation applies for a patent in foreign signatory nation, the inventor is treated in the same manner as inventors who live in the foreign nation. A treaty also provides patent applicants with the right of priority which gives the applicant filing application for a patent in one signatory nation the right to apply for protection in all other signatory nations, within a certain period of time. The United States is signatory to a priority treaty with China-Taiwan, Thailand and India that have rules similar to those of the Paris Convention. Inventors who file patent applications in the United States may also file in each of these countries within one-year and receive the benefit of reciprocal priority rights, the U.S. filing date and vice versa. A cross reference of countries that are members of treaties with the United States is shown at Appendix V.

The Paris Convention

The treaty known as the Paris Convention for the Protection of Industrial Property is also known simply as the Paris Convention. The Paris Convention is the oldest international patent treaty. It is comprised of 140 nations, including the United States as well as members of the European Patent Office (EPO) and members of the Patent Cooperation Treaty (PCT), as listed in Appendix III (Member Nations of the Paris Convention). Members of the Paris Convention and other international treaties do not consist solely of individual countries, but may include organizations and groups of countries that are referred to as member jurisdictions rather than member nations or member countries. The EPO, for example, is considered a single signatory to the convention. The treaty specifies that each jurisdiction or country of the treaty guarantee the citizens of the other countries the same patent and trademark rights that govern their own country. Patent applicants must make application in each signatory nation for which patent protection is sought. However, the treaty gives patent filers the right of priority with regard to patents, trademarks, and industrial designs. The right of priority gives the applicant who files application for a patent in one signatory nation the right to apply for protection in all other signatory nations within 12 months. It should be noted that the time for the right of priority is six months for industrial designs and trademarks. Subsequently filed applications are regarded as being filed on the same date of the first filed application and are also given priority over any applications filed for the same invention by another applicant. Further, subsequently filed applications cannot be invalidated by acts, such as publication, invention exploitation, trademark use, or the sale of copies of a design that occur within the time interval allowed to file subsequent applications in other countries. Each filing must be made in the language of the country in which coverage is sought with the exception of applications filed with the EPO. The EPO accepts applications filed in English. Separate filing fees must be paid to each member country.

The Patent Cooperation Treaty

The World Intellectual Property Organization (WIPO), located in Geneva, administers the Patent Cooperation Treaty (PCT). The PCT is inclusive of more than 90 nations, including the United States, as listed at Appendix IV (Member Nations of the Patent Cooperation Treaty). All member nations of the PCT are also members of the Paris Convention, but not vice versa. The PCT provides, among other things, that centralized filing procedures are followed and a standardized application format be used to file an international patent application for the same invention in each signatory nation. An applicant is required to file a separate application in each country or territory (such as the EPO) where patent coverage is desired The filing date documented for an initial international application is documented as the filing date for each international application filed for the same patent in a signatory nation. The international filing date offers the benefit of providing the date associated with the patent search of the invention and it also provides a later time period within which a national application must be filed. Another advantage of filing a PCT application is that an initial international patent search is conducted and PCT signatory nations are most likely to rely solely upon this patent search, simplifying the international patent process. A U.S. inventor must obtain a PCT foreign-filing license or wait until six months have elapsed since making application in the United States to make application in another PCT nation, The inventor may then delay the application process by 20 or 30 months, dependent upon whether the inventor makes request for examination under a provision known as Chapter 11 of the PCT. If an applicant requests such an examination before making application with nations of the PCT, Chapter 11 specifies that an inventor may select either the PTO or EPO to perform the patent examination.

Within 22 months of the filing date of a U.S. application or within three months of transmittal of a search report, the patent owner must elect to make use of Chapter 11. If the EPO is selected, the inventor must file application in Germany and make payment of the required fees in Deutschmarks, the German currency. Also, the inventor must file in non-EPO nations and the EPO within 20 months of the U.S. filing date. If an inventor files in a member country of the Paris Convention that is not a member of the PCT, the inventor is required to acquire a patent agent licensed to file under the particular country's patent laws. The patent filing requirements vary among countries, but most all have specific formats for drawings. A foreign agent or a company that specializes in making drawings for U.S. divisional applications may be sought to prepare the drawings. Foreign agents will require a power of attorney and a certified copy of the of the U.S. application from the PTO.

After filing a PCT application, the inventor receives an examination report from either the chosen PTO or EPO, The examination report will indicate which claims are allowed and which are rejected. The inventor may then make one amendment to the application and submit a statement responding to the issues. The inventor is also allowed to interview the patent examiner. Eventually, the patent examiner issues a final and formal determination of allowance or rejection. Whether the initial application is allowed or rejected, an inventor may file application in any PCT nation or jurisdiction before 30 months have expired. Each country and jurisdiction will rely heavily on the international examination that is issued by the PCT's International Bureau.

The PCT application differs from a U.S. application in format even though either format may be used for U.S. applications. Differences exist in the standards required for drawing size, margins, locations of page numbers and line spacing. When filing a PCT application, the inventor is also required to file a request form (form PTO/PCT/RO/101) and transmittal letter (form PTO 1382). The WIPO provides a method of filing a PCT application using its software package, PCT-Easy, which may be acquired through the WIPO Web site at **http://pcteasy.wipo.com**. The software automates the filing process and requires reduced fees for the filing. Inventors are encouraged to file a PCT application at least one month before the one-year expiration of the U.S. filing date. However, inventors may mail a PCT application as late as the last day of the one-year expiration of the U.S. filing date provided the inventor makes use of Express Mail and the Express Mail Certification is located on the first page of the transmittal letter. In return, the inventor receives a filing receipt and a serial number separate from the international application. The application is then transmitted to appropriate and designated countries and jurisdictions named on the inventor's request form. Inventors are allowed to make minor modifications to errors in the PCT application and are given one month to correct them. After a PCT search report is issued from either the PTO or EPO as designated by Chapter 11, the inventor is given one opportunity to comment on the report and amend the claims, but no extended prosecution or negotiation is allowed.

The European Patent Convention

The European Patent Convention (EPC) was created in support of the EPO, which is located in Munich, Germany. The EPO is a trilingual patent office, which grants Europatents that are good in all member countries of the EPC. EPO members include the following 31 states, listed by country code at Table 3.

AT – Austria	EE – Estonia	IS – Iceland	PL – Poland
BE – Belgium	ES – Spain	IT - Italy	PT – Portugal
BG – Bulgaria	FI – Finland	LI - Liechtenstein	RO - Romania
CH – Switzerland	FR – France	LT - Lithuania	SE – Sweden
CY – Cyprus	GB - United Kingdom	LU - Luxembourg	SI - Slovenia
CZ - Czech Republic	GR - Hellenic Republic	LV – Latvia	SK – Slovakia
DE – Germany	HU – Hungary	MC - Monaco	TR – Turkey
DK – Denmark	IE – Ireland	NL - Netherlands	

Table 3 – Member Nations of the European Patent Convention

The following states are affiliated with the EPO in the manner specified at Table 4.

Extension states that recognize European Patents
AL – Albania
BA – Bosnia and Herzegovina
HR – Croatia
MK – the former Yugoslav Republic of Macedonia
YU – Serbia and Montenegro (formerly known as the Federal Republic of Yugoslavia)
States entitled to accede to the EPC in accordance with article 166 EPC
NO – Norway
States invited to accede to the EPC
HR – Croatia
MK – the former Yugoslav Republic of Macedonia
MT – Malta

Table 4 - Affiliates of the EPC

The EPC is considered to be the same as a single country under the Paris Convention and the PCT. As such, a U.S. inventor may file application for a patent with the EPO and have the effective filing date documented as the date of filing in the United States, provided the EPO filing occurs within one year of the U.S. filing.

The EPO differs from the PTO in its patent examination procedures. The EPO requires patent examiners to be capable of speaking and writing at least three languages fluently and patent examiners take the initiative to offer suggestions on documenting claims such that claims are more likely to be allowed. The EPO publishes patent applications for opposition 18 months after filing application and requires that a maintenance fee be paid during the pendency period of the application. After an inventor has filed application for a patent with the EPO and had a Europatent issued for the invention, the inventor may register and file translations of the patent in individual EPC member nations without having those individual patent offices engage a separate review of the application. Inventors who are not residents of EPO member countries are required to file application with the EPO via a European patent agent. A granted Europatent is automatically valid in each EPC member country for which a patent application is designated, registered and for which the patent owner has filed translations and appointed a patent agent. A Europatent has a life of 20 years from the date of filing application, provided assessed maintenance fees are paid in the selected member countries.

Inventors are cautioned to consider the potential for profit and assess the necessity of establishing a patent in a foreign nation before making application. Laws pertaining to the filing of a patent application in foreign nations can be complicated, particularly in nations not governed by treaties with the United States. If it is determined that a foreign patent is necessitated in non-treaty nations, a number of patent attorneys that specialize in foreign patents are available to assist in making application. U.S.

law dictates that if an invention is made in the United States, a license must be obtained from the PTO before filing for a foreign patent if the foreign patent application is being filed before a U.S. application is filed or before six months have expired since the U.S. filing. By filing application for a U.S. patent, the inventor automatically requests such a license. The grant or denial of such a request is indicated in the filing receipt mailed to each patent applicant. If six months has passed since the filing of a U.S. patent, no license is necessary to file for a foreign patent unless the invention has been ordered kept secret. If the invention is ordered kept secret by a U.S. authoritarian body, consent from the PTO must be obtained to file a foreign patent during the period the order is in effect. The most common process used to acquire global patent rights is outlined below:

1. File in the United States.

2. File in non-member countries of the Paris Convention Treaty before publication or sale of the invention.

3. Under the Paris Convention Treaty, file a PCT application to cover PCT countries and jurisdictions within one year of filing with non-member countries of the Paris Convention.

4. Select the PTO or EPO to conduct the patent search.

5. File national applications with the EPO and non-EPO PCT countries within 30 months from the U.S. filing date, preferably with the assistance of foreign patent agents.

Foreign Applicants for U.S. Patents

The United States makes no distinction as to who may file application for a patent. Any person or entity may file application for a patent on the same basis as U.S. citizens, regardless of citizenship.

U.S. patent laws, which establish that each patent application and oath or declaration must be signed by the inventor, extend to citizens of foreign nations in contrast to many foreign patent laws, which have no requirement for the signature of the inventor, an oath, or a declaration. U.S. patent laws establish that no U.S. patent may be issued if the inventor, the inventor's legal representative, or an assignee is issued a foreign patent before making application in the United States. Also no U.S. patent may be issued if the inventor or the inventor's legal representative accepts assignment on application more than six months before filing application for a design patent and more than 12 months before filing all other types of patent applications in the United States.

An applicant who has previously regularly filed application for an invention in a foreign nation, which grants similar privileges to U.S. citizens, will have the same effect for the purpose of overcoming intervening acts of others, as if the application were filed in the United States on the same date on which the application for the same invention was filed in that foreign nation. The U.S. application must be filed within six months from the earliest date on which the foreign design patent was filed or within 12 months for all other types of patents. To secure this right of priority, the applicant must obtain a certified copy of the foreign patent application from the patent office of the foreign nation in which the patent was filed. If an application has been filed or assigned in a foreign nation prior to filing application in the United States, the oath or declaration of the U.S. application must attest to the earliest such country in which a patent application was previously filed and any other country in which a patent application was filed more than one year prior to the U.S. filing date. The date of filing such foreign applications must also be specified in the oath or declaration of the patent filed in the United States.

An oath or declaration is required of all inventors making

application for U.S. patents or any legal representative making application on behalf of the inventor. When the applicant is in the United States, the oath must be notarized and signed before a notary public or other party authorized to perform notary functions. When an applicant is in a foreign nation, the oath may be may be sworn before any diplomatic, any consular of the U.S. or any officer having an official seal, who is authorized to administer oaths in the particular country and whose proof of such authority is certified by a certificate of a diplomatic or consular officer of the U.S. An oath must contain the official seal of the officer before which the oath is made.

An oath taken before an officer of a foreign nation and all application papers, with the exception of drawings, must be attached with a ribbon that is passed one or more times through each sheet of the papers. The ends of the ribbon must be brought together under the seal before the seal is affixed or impressed or each sheet must be impressed with the official seal. When a declaration is made in lieu of an oath, the applicant need not appear before an official and the application papers need not be attached with a ribbon.

Any patent agent or attorney who is registered to practice before the PTO may represent a foreign patent applicant.

chapter eleven

Parts of a Patent Application

The filing of a patent application can be quite complex and detail-intensive. However, it is not impossible for a layperson to complete and file the application on his or her own. When filing a patent application, there are three main considerations: the specifications, the main claims, and the advantages of the invention. The specification provides a description of the invention and its associated drawings as well as the details of the operation of the invention and drawings. The specification should provide enough detail that a person skilled in the art of the invention would be capable of making and using the invention based solely upon the information documented in the specification. The main claims of the invention should be as broad as any associated prior art permits the claims to be. The advantages of the invention should be definitive enough to sell the invention. Though there are three main considerations for filing a patent application, the application requires much more documentation. The other parts of the application are considered to be of lesser importance.

All of the parts of a patent application should be prepared and sent together as a single package. PTO rules require that elements or parts of a patent application should be arranged in a specific order with headings in capital letters. However, the rules do not prevent applicants from adding headers, particularly if the content of the application is long or technically complex. It is recommended that any additional headers be inserted with the first letter of the header capitalized. The following parts of a patent application are listed in the order required by PTO rules. Required headers are listed in all capital letters.

Receipt Postcard

The application should include a self-addressed receipt postcard so that the inventor is assured that the PTO receives the patent application. The back of card should include the following information:

- The inventor's name.

- The title of the invention.

- The number of drawing sheets included.

- The total number of pages in the specification, claims, and abstract.

- The patent application declaration with the number of pages and signature date.

- An indication of whether a patent application transmittal, fee transmittal, credit card payment form, or check is included. If a check is included, the check number and amount should be specified.

- An indication of whether a non-publication request is included.

   Applicants should leave enough space at the bottom of the back of the postcard to allow the PTO to affix its sticker to the postcard. The PTO will affix a sticker that indicates the date of receipt at the PTO and the serial number assigned to the particular patent application. Inventors must be sure to include enough postage for the postcard to be returned.

Payment

Payment may be made by check, money order, or credit card. If a credit card is used for payment, the applicant must include a completed Form PTO-2038 to cover the filing fee.

Transmittal Letter

A transmittal letter is used to indicate to the PT which parts of the patent application are being sent. A transmittal letter for a design patent is shown in Figure 1.

Fee Transmittal

The PTO uses the fee transmittal form to compute and verify the filing fee. A fee transmittal form is shown in Figure 2.

Non-Publication Request

A non-publication request instructs the PTO not to publish the patent application. This request is usually made to protect trade secret rights, and it also eliminates the need to pay the publication fee. A non-publication request form is shown in Figure 3.

Drawings

Patent laws require that drawings be furnished with patent applications whenever a drawing is necessary to understand the invention. It is not uncommon for patents classified as compositions of matter or processes to be submitted without drawings because the subject matter may not require such a demonstration. Submitted drawings must detail every feature described in the claims. The PTO establishes standards for submitted drawings so that they are capable of being printed and published in an organized form that is easily understood. Though the PTO insists upon complying with its established standards for drawings, an application will not be returned for failing to comply with drawing standards. Instead, the PTO will accept the application for examination and require that the applicant submit a new or corrected drawing at a later time. Failure to submit a compliant drawing later may lead to rejection. Applicants are encouraged to engage the services of a competent draftsman to ensure that drawings are created in compliance with established standards. Standards specify the following characteristics for drawings:

PTO/SB/18 (07-06)
Approved for use through 01/31/2007. OMB 0651-0032
U.S. Patent and Trademark Office; U.S. DEPARTMENT OF COMMERCE
Under the Paperwork Reduction Act of 1995, no persons are required to respond to a collection of information unless it displays a valid OMB control number.

DESIGN
PATENT APPLICATION
TRANSMITTAL

(Only for new nonprovisional applications under 37 CFR 1.53(b))

Attorney Docket No.	
First Named Inventor	
Title	
Express Mail Label No.	

ADDRESS TO:
Commissioner for Patents
P.O. Box 1450
Alexandria, VA 22313-1450

DESIGN V. UTILITY: A "design patent" protects an article's ornamental appearance (e.g., the way an article looks) (35 U.S.C. 171), while a "utility patent" protects the way an article is used and works (35 U.S.C. 101). The ornamental appearance of an article includes its shape/configuration or surface ornamentation upon the article, or both. Both a design and a utility patent may be obtained on an article if invention resides both in its ornamental appearance and its utility. For more information, see MPEP 1502.01.

APPLICATION ELEMENTS
See MPEP 1500 concerning design patent application contents.

1. ☐ Fee Transmittal Form *(e.g., PTO/SB/17)*
   (Submit an original, and a duplicate for fee processing)

2. ☐ Applicant claims small entity status.
   See 37 CFR 1.27.

3. ☐ Specification   [Total Pages _____]
   (preferred arrangement set forth below, MPEP 1503.01)
   - Preamble
   - Cross References to Related Applications
   - Statement Regarding Fed sponsored R & D
   - Description of the figure(s) of the drawings
   - Feature description
   - Claim (only one (1) claim permitted, MPEP 1503.03)

4. ☐ Drawing(s) *(37 CFR 1.152)* [Total Sheets _____]

5. Oath or Declaration   [Total Pages _____]

   a. ☐ Newly executed (original or copy)

   b. ☐ A copy from a prior application (37 CFR 1.63(d))
      (for continuation/divisional with Box 16 completed)
      DELETION OF INVENTOR(S)
      i. ☐ Signed statement attached deleting inventor(s) named in the prior application, see 37 CFR 1.63(d)(2) and 1.33(b)

6. ☐ Application Data Sheet. See 37 CFR 1.76

ACCOMPANYING APPLICATION PARTS

7. ☐ Assignment Papers (cover sheet & document(s))

8. ☐ 37 CFR 3.73(b) Statement   ☐ Power of
   (when there is an assignee)   Attorney

9. ☐ English Translation Document *(if applicable)*

10. ☐ Information Disclosure Statement (IDS)
    PTO/SB/08 or PTO-1449
    ☐ Copies of foreign patent documents, publications, & other information

11. ☐ Preliminary Amendment

12. ☐ Return Receipt Postcard (MPEP 503)
    (Should be specifically itemized)

13. ☐ Certified Copy of Priority Document(s)
    (if foreign priority is claimed)

14. ☐ Request for Expedited Examination of a Design Application
    (37 CFR 1.155) (NOTE: Use "Mail Stop Expedited Design")

15. ☐ Other:

16. If a CONTINUING APPLICATION, check appropriate box, and supply the requisite information below and in the first sentence of the specification following the title, or in an Application Data Sheet under 37 CFR 1.76:

☐ Continuation   ☐ Divisional   ☐ Continuation-in-part (CIP) of prior application No.: _____

Prior application information: Examiner _____   Art Unit: _____

17. CORRESPONDENCE ADDRESS

☐ The address associated with Customer Number: _____   **OR**   ☐ Correspondence address below

Name	
Address	

City		State		Zip Code	
Country		Telephone		Email	

Signature	Date
Name (Print/Type)	Registration No. (Attorney/Agent)

This collection of information is required by 37 CFR 1.53(b). The information is required to obtain or retain a benefit by the public which is to file (and by the USPTO to process) an application. Confidentiality is governed by 35 U.S.C. 122 and 37 CFR 1.11 and 1.14. This collection is estimated to take 12 minutes to complete, including gathering, preparing, and submitting the completed application form to the USPTO. Time will vary depending upon the individual case. Any comments on the amount of time you require to complete this form and/or suggestions for reducing this burden, should be sent to the Chief Information Officer, U.S. Patent and Trademark Office, U.S. Department of Commerce, P.O. Box 1450, Alexandria, VA 22313-1450. DO NOT SEND FEES OR COMPLETED FORMS TO THIS ADDRESS. **SEND TO: Commissioner for Patents, P.O. Box 1450, Alexandria, VA 22313-1450.**
If you need assistance in completing the form, call 1-800-PTO-9199 and select option 2.

Figure 1 - Design Patent Transmittal Letter

PTO/SB/17 (07-06)
Approved for use through 01/31/2007. OMB 0651-0032
U.S. Patent and Trademark Office; U.S. DEPARTMENT OF COMMERCE
Under the Paperwork Reduction Act of 1995 no persons are required to respond to a collection of information unless it displays a valid OMB control number

Effective on 12/08/2004. Fees pursuant to the Consolidated Appropriations Act, 2005 (H.R. 4818). **FEE TRANSMITTAL For FY 2006** ☐ Applicant claims small entity status. See 37 CFR 1.27 **TOTAL AMOUNT OF PAYMENT** ($)	**Complete if Known**
	Application Number
	Filing Date
	First Named Inventor
	Examiner Name
	Art Unit
	Attorney Docket No.

METHOD OF PAYMENT (check all that apply)

☐ Check ☐ Credit Card ☐ Money Order ☐ None ☐ Other (please identify): _____

☐ Deposit Account   Deposit Account Number: _____   Deposit Account Name: _____

For the above-identified deposit account, the Director is hereby authorized to: (check all that apply)

☐ Charge fee(s) indicated below   ☐ Charge fee(s) indicated below, **except for the filing fee**

☐ Charge any additional fee(s) or underpayments of fee(s) under 37 CFR 1.16 and 1.17   ☐ Credit any overpayments

WARNING: Information on this form may become public. Credit card information should not be included on this form. Provide credit card information and authorization on PTO-2038.

FEE CALCULATION

1. BASIC FILING, SEARCH, AND EXAMINATION FEES

	FILING FEES		SEARCH FEES		EXAMINATION FEES		
Application Type	Fee ($)	Small Entity Fee ($)	Fee ($)	Small Entity Fee ($)	Fee ($)	Small Entity Fee ($)	Fees Paid ($)
Utility	300	150	500	250	200	100	_____
Design	200	100	100	50	130	65	_____
Plant	200	100	300	150	160	80	_____
Reissue	300	150	500	250	600	300	_____
Provisional	200	100	0	0	0	0	_____

2. EXCESS CLAIM FEES

Fee Description	Fee ($)	Small Entity Fee ($)
Each claim over 20 (including Reissues)	50	25
Each independent claim over 3 (including Reissues)	200	100
Multiple dependent claims	360	180

Total Claims	Extra Claims	Fee ($)	Fee Paid ($)		Multiple Dependent Claims	
_____ - 20 or HP = _____	x _____	= _____			Fee ($)	Fee Paid ($)
HP = highest number of total claims paid for, if greater than 20.					_____	_____

Indep. Claims	Extra Claims	Fee ($)	Fee Paid ($)
_____ - 3 or HP = _____	x _____	= _____	
HP = highest number of independent claims paid for, if greater than 3.			

3. APPLICATION SIZE FEE

If the specification and drawings exceed 100 sheets of paper (excluding electronically filed sequence or computer listings under 37 CFR 1.52(e)), the application size fee due is $250 ($125 for small entity) for each additional 50 sheets or fraction thereof. See 35 U.S.C. 41(a)(1)(G) and 37 CFR 1.16(s).

Total Sheets	Extra Sheets	Number of each additional 50 or fraction thereof	Fee ($)	Fee Paid ($)
_____ - 100 = _____	/ 50 = _____	(round up to a whole number) x _____		= _____

4. OTHER FEE(S)

Non-English Specification, $130 fee (no small entity discount)   Fees Paid ($) _____

Other (e.g., late filing surcharge): _____   _____

SUBMITTED BY

Signature		Registration No. (Attorney/Agent)	Telephone	
Name (Print/Type)			Date	

This collection of information is required by 37 CFR 1.136. The information is required to obtain or retain a benefit by the public which is to file (and by the USPTO to process) an application. Confidentiality is governed by 35 U.S.C. 122 and 37 CFR 1.14. This collection is estimated to take 30 minutes to complete, including gathering, preparing, and submitting the completed application form to the USPTO. Time will vary depending upon the individual case. Any comments on the amount of time you require to complete this form and/or suggestions for reducing this burden, should be sent to the Chief Information Officer, U.S. Patent and Trademark Office, U.S. Department of Commerce, P.O. Box 1450, Alexandria, VA 22313-1450. DO NOT SEND FEES OR COMPLETED FORMS TO THIS ADDRESS. **SEND TO: Commissioner for Patents, P.O. Box 1450, Alexandria, VA 22313-1450.**

If you need assistance in completing the form, call 1-800-PTO-9199 and select option 2.

Figure 2 - Fee Transmittal Form

PTO/SB/35 (09-06)
Approved for use through 03/31/2007. OMB 0651-0031
U.S. Patent and Trademark Office; U. S. DEPARTMENT OF COMMERCE
Under the Paperwork Reduction Act of 1995, no persons are required to respond to a collection of information unless it displays a valid OMB control number.

NONPUBLICATION REQUEST UNDER 35 U.S.C. 122(b)(2)(B)(i)	First Named Inventor	
	Title	
	Attorney Docket Number	

I hereby certify that the invention disclosed in the attached application **has not and will not be** the subject of an application filed in another country, or under a multilateral international agreement, that requires publication at eighteen months after filing.

I hereby request that the attached application not be published under 35 U.S.C. 122(b).

_____   _____
Signature   Date

_____   _____
Typed or printed name   Registration Number, if applicable

_____
Telephone Number

This request must be signed in compliance with 37 CFR 1.33(b) and submitted with the application **upon filing.**

Applicant may rescind this nonpublication request at any time. If applicant rescinds a request that an application not be published under 35 U.S.C. 122(b), the application will be scheduled for publication at eighteen months from the earliest claimed filing date for which a benefit is claimed.

If applicant subsequently files an application directed to the invention disclosed in the attached application in another country, or under a multilateral international agreement, that requires publication of applications eighteen months after filing, the applicant **must** notify the United States Patent and Trademark Office of such filing within forty-five (45) days after the date of the filing of such foreign or international application. **Failure to do so will result in abandonment of this application (35 U.S.C. 122(b)(2)(B)(iii)).**

This collection of information is required by 37 CFR 1.213(a). The information is required to obtain or retain a benefit by the public which is to file (and by the USPTO to process) an application. Confidentiality is governed by 35 U.S.C. 122 and 37 CFR 1.11 and 1.14. This collection is estimated to take 6 minutes to complete, including gathering, preparing, and submitting the completed application form to the USPTO. Time will vary depending upon the individual case. Any comments on the amount of time you require to complete this form and/or suggestions for reducing this burden, should be sent to the Chief Information Officer, U.S. Patent and Trademark Office, U.S. Department of Commerce, P.O. Box 1450, Alexandria, VA 22313-1450. DO NOT SEND FEES OR COMPLETED FORMS TO THIS ADDRESS. **SEND TO: Commissioner for Patents, P.O. Box 1450, Alexandria, VA 22313-1450.**

If you need assistance in completing the form, call 1-800-PTO-9199 (1-800-786-9199) and select option 2.

Figure 3 – Non-Publication Request Form

Ink and Print

Black or India ink on white paper with solid black lines or colored drawings is required for utility patents. Colored drawings are only acceptable when it is the only practical medium by which the invention may be disclosed. The PTO must grant the inventor a petition that explains that colored drawings are necessary. The petition must be accompanied by appropriate fees, three sets of colored drawings, and the following language, placed at the first paragraph of the brief description of the drawing in the specification. "The file of this patent contains at least one drawing executed in color. Copies of this patent with color drawing(s) will be provided by the Patent and Trademark Office upon request and payment of the necessary fee."

Shading

All lines, numbers, and letters must be durable, uniformly thick, sufficiently dense and weighted to allow for adequate reproduction. This is inclusive of lines, numbers, and letters that are purposely included with varying thicknesses. Shading is encouraged to aid in the understanding of an invention, particularly when the shading is used to illustrate parts in perspective. However, shading must not reduce legibility and it is not recommended for illustrating cross sections. Solid black shading is not allowed except when used in bar graphs. Shading should be accomplished with the use of thin, spaced lines with as few lines as practical for the illustration. As an alternative to shading, heavy lines may be used for the shaded side of objects. The lines must not superimpose on each other or obscure any reference characters. Light should extend from the upper left corner of the page at a 45° angle.

Letters, Numbers, and Reference Characters

The English alphabet should be used for lettering, except where it is customary to use the lettering of another language. The lettering must be customary in the particular field of art, such as the Greek symbolism typically used in mathematics and other scientific fields. Numbers, letters, and reference characters must be presented in the same orientation as the view so that the page does not have to be rotated to view them. It is preferred that reference characters be presented as numerals. Reference characters, view numbers, and sheet numbers must be presented in plain, legible type. They must appear distinct and conform to the following standards:

- Measure at least ⅛ inch in height.

- Not cross or mingle lines of the drawing.

- Not be placed atop hatched or shaded surfaces.

- Not be used with brackets, inverted commas, or encircled with lines.

The same reference number must be used to represent the same part of the invention when that part is presented in different views. An existing reference number may never be used to designate or reference another part. Reference numbers may not exist in a drawing if they are not mentioned in the specification and vice versa.

Lead lines are the straight or curved lines used to link reference characters to the particular object being referenced. Lead lines should be as short as necessary to make the link and they may not cross each other. Each lead line should originate in the immediate proximity of the reference character and extend to the object of reference. An arrow may be placed at the end of the lead line. If the arrow is a free-standing arrow, the arrow indicates the entire section that it points to. If the arrow makes contact with a line of a surface, the arrow indicates the particular surface that it touches. Any other arrow presented in the drawing is used to show direction of movement. A lead line is required for each reference character except when reference characters are used to indicate surfaces or cross sections. In such instances, reference characters are placed atop the surface or cross section to which it refers and the reference character must be underlined to indicate that a lead line was not purposely left out.

Symbols

Symbols and other labeled representations must be defined in the specification. Known devices should be illustrated by universally recognized symbols that have conventional meanings and are generally recognized in the particular field of art. The PTO must approve the use of other symbols. The PTO will generally allow the use of symbols that are not universally recognized if they are not likely to be confused with conventional symbols and if they are readily identifiable.

Graphic Forms

Mathematical formula, chemical formula, tables, and waveforms that are provided in graphic form may be submitted as drawings. Each graphic form must be labeled as a separate figure. Formula must include brackets, when necessary, to show proper integration. Waveforms must share a common vertical axis with time parameters along the horizontal axis. The figure must correspond to the definition included in the specification and be identified by a letter designation placed adjacent to the vertical axis.

Photographs

Black and white photographs are allowed for utility and design patents only after the PTO grants a petition requesting that photographs be accepted. The appropriate fees and three sets of photographs must accompany the petition. Colored photographs will also be accepted for utility patents if the conditions for color drawings are satisfied. (See Ink Section.) Photographs must be developed on double-weight photo paper or permanently bound Bristol board. The quality of the photographs must be such that they are reproducible for the printed patent.

Paper Size

All submitted drawings must be of the same size, either size A4 or 8½ by 11 inches. Size A4 paper is 21.0 cm. x 29.7 cm. Paper size 8 ½ x 11 is equivalent to 21.6 cm. x 27.9 cm. The shorter measurement is always regarded as the top and bottom width of the paper.

Type of Paper

Drawings must be placed on white, flexible, smooth, non-glossy, durable paper. The paper must be free of creases, folds, cracks, alterations, over-writings, and interlineations. It must also be reasonably free of erasures. Drawings must be placed only on one side of the paper. Photographs must be developed on double-weight photo paper or permanently mounted on Bristol board as discussed under "Photographs," above. The applicant should place no holes on a drawing.

Margins

Each page of the drawing must include margins of at least one inch on the top and left side, at least $9/16$ inches on the right side and at least $3/8$ inches at the bottom. 1 inch = 2.5 cm., $9/16$ inches = 1.5 cm. and $3/8$ inches = 1.0 cm. Using these standards for margins, the actual drawing may be displayed in a maximum area of 17.0 cm. X 26.2 cm using A4 sized paper and 17.6 cm. x 24.4 cm. using 8½ X 11 sized paper. While drawings must conform to these established standards for margins, they may not contain borders.

Numbering

The sheets of a drawing should be consecutively numbered and each sheet should be identified using two Arabic numerals situated on either side of an oblique line. The first number represents the sheet number, and it should represent a consecutive order staring with the numeral one. The second number represents the total number of sheets included in the drawing. The sheet number should be placed at the top center of the sheet, but it must not be placed within the established margins of the page. If a drawing consumes much of the drawing area and extends too far to the top of the drawing area, the sheet number may be placed on the right hand side of the drawing. Two avoid confusion with numbers used as reference characters; sheet numbers are required to be larger than reference numbers.

Views of a drawing must also be numbered in consecutive order using Arabic numerals beginning with the number one. View numbers are independent of sheet numbers and should correspond to the order in which views appear on the drawing sheets. When partial views are used to represent a single part, the exact same number must identify each view. Each view number must be preceded by the term "FIG" and followed by a capital letter. View numbers may not include brackets, circles, or inverted commas and they must be larger than any numbers used as reference characters. If only a single view is used in a patent application, it does not need to be numbered or identified by the term "FIG."

Drawing Identification

No identifying information, such as a name, is allowed on a drawing itself. However, each drawing must have some type of identification placed on the back of the drawing page. Identifying information should include the patent application number or the title of the invention. Identifying information may also contain the patent attorney's name, phone, and docket number, or the inventor's name, phone, and case number. The PTO uses contact information in the case that drawings cannot be matched properly to the correct patent application. Identifying information should be placed at a minimum of ⅝ inches from the top of the back of the page with a reference to the patent application number. If a patent application number has not yet been assigned, the inventor's name should be placed in the left hand corner of the back of the sheet. The sheet number and total number of sheets of drawings may be specified on the front of the page as follows, "Sheet 6 of 13."

Views

Drawings must include as many views of an invention as necessary to show it properly. All views must be grouped together and arranged in portrait position, preferably. For some inventions it may be more advantageous to place a view in landscape position for illustration purposes. With such views the top margin is rotated to the right hand side of the page, and words must be readable from left to right with the exception of those words that are angled and rotated for charts and graphs. More than one view may be contained on a single page so long as they are clearly separated from one another and the arrangement of views does not waste space. Views must not be placed atop one another or within the outline of each other.

Views must not contain centerline, and projection lines may not be used to connect views. If views contain waveforms that need to demonstrate a connection, they may be connected with the use of dashed lines. Views may be used to represent plans, elevations, perspectives, and sections as well as larger or smaller scales. At least one view must be complete and suitable for publication in the Official Gazette for patents as the preferred illustration of the invention.

Exploded Views

Exploded views, which show the relationship of parts or the order of assembly of parts, should have the separated parts embraced by brackets. When an exploded view is placed on a page with more than one figure, brackets should embrace the exploded view.

Partial Views

Partial views are necessary when a device or machine is large and requires several views to show it properly or requires partial views spread among more than one page. The relationship between partial views must be clear and unambiguous, and there should be no loss in facility of understanding the view. No two partial views should contain the same components of the whole view. Partial views should be capable of being linked edge to edge so that no overlap occurs. The whole view, formed by the partial views, should be shown on a smaller scale. When any portion of a partial view is exploded, the partial and exploded views must be labeled as separate views.

Sectional Views

Sectional views show a particular section of a view. A broken line should indicate the section being viewed. The endpoints of the broken line must indicate the view number of the sectional view and be designated by either Roman or Arabic numerals. An arrow must be included to indicate the direction of sight. The plane upon which the section is taken must also be indicated on the view. Hatched lines must be used to fill the section. Hatched lines must be at a substantial angle (preferably 45°) to the surrounding axes or to the principal lines. Hatched lines must include regularly spaced, oblique, parallel lines. Spacing should be sufficient to distinguish the lines and the hatching should not impede the ability to see reference characters and lead lines. If reference characters are not situated outside of the hatched area, the hatching must be spaced around the characters.

Cross Section Views

A cross section of a view must be drawn out to show all of the materials as they exist in the view. Hatched lines that are regularly spaced by parallel oblique strokes must fill all parts in the cross section. The spacing of the strokes should remain consistent for each part of a cross section taken from the same item. The spacing forms the basis for the entire area to be hatched. Different types of hatching should convey different materials in the cross section. The hatching of juxtaposed different elements must be angled differently. Large areas may be hatched at the inside edging of the area. The hatching must be drawn to form an outline of the entire area

If a view must be represented in an alternate position, a broken line should be superimposed on the view, if it can be done without crowding the view; otherwise, a separate view must be drawn to represent the alternate position. If a form of construction is modified, it must be shown in a separate view.

Scale

The scale of drawings must be sufficient to show a mechanism without causing the drawing to be crowded when it is reduced to ⅔ of its size by reproduction. Large drawings may be presented in portions, using multiple sheets of paper when it is necessary to properly represent details. However, the number of sheets must be kept to a minimum and the space on the sheet must not be wasteful. The scale of each drawing may only be indicated at the request of a PTO examiner. Indications of scale, such as "actual size" or " one half scale" may lose their meaning when the drawing is reproduced and reduced in size. Elements of the same view must be presented in proportion, unless a difference is proportion serves to increase the clarity of the view. Rather than showing elements of the same view in different proportion, an additional view may be included that shows the element at a larger scale. A finely drawn line or a dot-dash circle must surround the element being enlarged by the additional view without obstructing the view.

Legends

Descriptive legends may be used to aid in the understanding of a drawing. In some circumstances, the PTO may require that legends be included and subject such legends to approval. Legends should include as few words as is practical to understand a particular drawing.

Copyright Notice or Mask Work Notice

When copyrighted or mask work material is included in a drawing, a copyright notice or mask work notice must appear within site of the drawing. The notice must be placed immediately below the material to which it refers. The content of the notice must be limited to those elements of the notice that are required by law. Copyright and mask work notices are only permitted on drawings when the appropriate authorization language is included at the beginning of the specification.

Security Markings

Any authorized security markings are required to be centered in the top margin of the drawing sheet.

Specification

A specification includes a written description of the invention and the manner and process of using or making it. The latter is what is known as patent claims. The specification that defines and discloses an invention must meet certain requirements. The specification must adhere to both the enabling rule and the best mode rule. The enabling rule requires that the language of the specification be clear, concise, and exact such that any person skilled in the particular technology or field of the invention, or any person skilled in a closely related field would be capable of interpreting and practicing the invention without extensive experimentation. The best mode rule requires that the specification disclose the best manner of carrying out the invention. The specification should describe the invention such that it is distinguishable from other inventions and from what is already known. The specification must describe the specific embodiment of the invention and the best mode of operation or the best process, as contemplated by the inventor. If the invention is an improvement over prior-art, the specification must point out the parts or processes that constitute an improvement. A specification includes the following sections:

Title

The first page of the specification should include the TITLE of the invention as a section header if the title is not otherwise presented at the beginning of the application. The title should contain no more than 500 characters in capital letters. No boldface characters or underlined characters are allowed.

Cross Reference to Related Applications

This section of the specification is used to claim priority of any provisional patent application or prior related applications that have been filed by the inventor. If no provisional application or related applications exist, the phrase "not applicable" should follow the header.

Federally Sponsored Research

If the invention was developed under a government contract and the government has rights to the invention, this section of the specification must indicate that relationship. If the government has rights to the invention, the phrase "not applicable" should follow the header.

Sequence Listing or Program

If a computer program or biotech sequence listing is included as an appendix to the patent application or if it is included on CD-ROM or on microfiche, that information should be indicated in this section. If no computer program or biotech sequence is included, the phrase "not applicable" should follow the header.

Background of the Invention

This section of the specification is used to indicate the technical field of the invention. The section includes two subsections, "prior art" and "objectives and advantages," as indicated below.

Prior Art

This subsection of the background of the invention is used to indicate any problems that the invention solves and discuss or criticize any relevant prior art in the technical field of the invention.

Objectives and Advantages

This subsection of the background of the invention is used to indicate all positive aspects of the invention.

Summary

This section should include a brief summary of the invention, which indicates the nature and substance of the invention, as claimed. The summary should define the objective of the invention.

Drawing Figures

This section of the specification provides a brief listing of all drawing figures supplied with the application. Optionally, this section may also include the subsection, reference numerals, but it is not required. If no drawings are included with the application, the phrase "not applicable" should follow the header.

Reference Numerals

Reference numerals are the numbers associated with drawings to designate the respective parts of the invention.

Detailed Description

The detailed description must define the parts or processes necessary to achieve and understand any improvement offered by the invention. It should describe the structure of the main embodiment of the invention. The description should be brief and make reference to any accompanying drawings provided with the application. The description should refer to different views of the invention and refer to each view by a figure number. The various parts of each figure should be referenced by numerals. If the application contains computer program that is fewer than about ten pages, its program listing may be included here or in the drawings. Longer programs should be listed in an appendix, stored on microfiche, or stored on CD-ROM.

The following sub-sections, Operation of Preferred Embodiment, Description of Additional Embodiment, Operation of Additional Embodiment and Conclusion, Ramification and Scope should be included in the detailed description section as warranted.

Operation of Preferred Embodiment

This sub-section of the detailed description explains how the main embodiment of the invention works or operates.

Description of Additional Embodiment

This sub-section of the detailed description describes the structure of an alternative embodiment that may exist. This subsection must be created for each additional embodiment of the invention.

Operation of Additional Embodiment

This sub-section of the detailed description describes the operation of any alternative embodiment. This subsection must be created for each additional embodiment of the invention.

Conclusion, Ramification, and Scope

This sub-section of the detailed description summarizes all advantages, alternative uses, and alternative physical forms of the invention. This sub-section should also include a broadening statement that indicates that the invention is not limited to the particular form or forms included.

Claims

The specification concludes with claims, which specify the subject matter applicable to the invention. Claims define the area of technology covered by the patent. As such, claims legally define the components, which are used to establish rights to an invention and the scope of protection that is sought for a patent. Claims establish the scope for which the courts judge infringement. Claims are of such importance in establishing rights to an invention that the inventor should draft them and submit them to a patent attorney for review and editing before filing a patent application. A patent attorney will convert the draft into legal form. Patent attorneys have the skills to develop the legal form of claims that gives them the broadest possible coverage that may be established.

Broad Claims

Broad claims provide the greatest patent protection so long as they are carefully written to avoid design-around. Design-around is basically designing a similar invention and manipulating the language of claims in an attempt to void the claims of the original invention. The terms, materials and composition, for example, may be used to offer broader coverage than the terms, wood or steel. Broad claims are vulnerable to subsequent improvements and the inventor must determine whether the improvement is more important than the original broad claim. The original broad claim for the ZipLoc® bag did not include the double and triple rails that are now standard in the bags. The double and triple rails were an improvement patent issued after the original patent. Because broad claims are more powerful than narrow claims and subsequent improvements, patents that contain broad claims are also referred to as dominant patents. Broad claims are usually presented as independent claims.

Narrow Claims

Narrow claims relate to specific inventive details of existing products. They commonly describe improvements to existing patents or existing product groups. Narrow claims do not have the breath of broad claims and are more vulnerable to design around. However, if they are used to represent a preferred technology or broad claims, their specificity can be powerful and valuable. An upright vacuum cleaner, for example, may be patented with a claim that defines a vacuum with one or more wheels. An improvement patent may claim a vacuum with four or more wheels that is self-propelled. The broad coverage of the original patent claim covers all two-wheeled and four-wheeled vacuum cleaners and electric brooms. On the other hand, the narrow coverage of the subsequent patent covers only four-wheeled self-propelled vacuums. It could be argued that the narrow claim of the subsequent patent is more valuable and powerful than the broad coverage provided by the original patent because the narrow claim insists upon self-propulsion.

Independent Claims

Independent claims are claims that stand alone, which implies that the description provided in the claim does not rely upon any other claim of the patent. Independent claims cover the broader inventive matter. A patent typically includes one to four independent claims. However, improvements may be included in the same patent application and documented as independent claims.

Dependent Claims

Dependent claims may be dependent upon one or more independent claims or they may be dependent upon one or more other dependent claims. When a dependent claim is dependent upon other dependent claims, the claim is considered to a multiple dependent claim. Dependent claims cover the more narrow inventive matter. Infringement may be based on infringing either the independent claims and/or infringing the dependent claims. As such, dependent claims assist in broadening the scope of patent protection.

Broad Patent Coverage

It is best that patent claims provide the broadest possible coverage for a patent. The broadest coverage is attained by including independent claims and also as many independent claims as possible. Documenting good patent claims is an expertise that may best be handled with the services of a patent attorney. One of the things that a good patent attorney should be capable of doing is making sure that an invention is protected with convincing patent claims. An experienced individual may easily overlook facets of the invention and apply for a patent that does not provide enough claims to protect the invention once it is patented. Even if a patent attorney includes more claims than are necessary, it is the job of the patent examiner to weed out claims that are obvious, too broad, or inclusive of prior art. Further, it is the job of the patent attorney to negotiate with the patent examiner on behalf of the inventor in an effort to acquire the broadest possible coverage. It is the strategy of some patent attorneys to include broad claims purposely and allow the patent examiner to decide which claims to reject. Once claims are written for submission, the inventor must review them to be sure that they accurately reflect the invention and give the patent attorney an opinion and approval for submission.

The specification of every patent application must be supported by one or more claims. Multiple claims must be substantially different from one another. Claims must be attributable to the invention as described in the specification. Terms and phrases used in claims must be easily defined by making reference to their definition and use, as provided in the description. Inventors should engage the services of a competent IP professional to develop the language of claims. There are three general types of claims: narrow claims, independent claims, and dependent claims, and the language contained must meet certain legal requirements. Claims may be presented in dependent form or as multiple dependent claims. Multiple dependent claims may not serve as the basis for other multiple dependent claims.

Sequence Listing

If the invention includes a nucleotide or amino acid sequence that the inventor wishes to document, it should be documented under this heading. If no such sequences are included with the invention, the phrase "not applicable" should follow the header.

Abstract

The specification should also include a brief abstract of the technical disclosure of that which is new to the art in which the invention pertains. The abstract should be included as a separate page immediately following the claims or the specification. The abstract should be presented as a single paragraph of fewer than 250 words entitled, "Abstract of the Disclosure."

Other Documents

Other documents that are required to complete a patent application are as follows.

Patent Application Declaration (PAD) Form

A Patent Application Declaration (PAD) form must be completed for each patent application. The form includes a statement under penalty of perjury that the inventor is the true inventor of the applied invention and that the inventor acknowledges the duty to keep the PTO informed of all prior art and other material information related to the invention. A PAD form is shown at Figure 4.

Disclosure Document Reference Letter

A Disclosure Reference Letter refers to any previously filed disclosure documents related to the invention being applied for.

Information Disclosure Statement and List of Prior Art

The Information Disclosure Statement and List of Prior Art cited by the applicant are technically not a part of a patent application, but the information contained within should be included in the patent application. However, these documents as well as copies of the listed prior art are expected to be submitted either in addition to the patent application or soon thereafter. These documents inform the PTO of all relevant prior art or any circumstances that have the potential to affect the novelty or non-obviousness of the invention applied for. When the patent is issued, the PTO will include information contained in these documents to the printed and issued patent.

Exhibits, Models, and Specimen

Generally, the language of the description, specification, and drawings provided with a patent application should suffice in defining an invention. However, in some rare instances, a model, exhibit, or specimen may be required to understand an invention completely. When such cases are necessary, a PTO examiner will request them. When a model is requested for a perpetual motion device, the applicant may be required to comply with the request by providing a working model of the invention. If the invention is a composition of matter, the applicant may be requested to provide a specimen of the composition, or the applicant may be requested to provide ingredients or intermediates of the composition for inspection or experimentation. If the invention is a microbiological source, the applicant may be required to provide a deposit of the microorganism that forms the basis for the invention.

Parts of the Provisional Patent Application

A provisional patent application (PPA) must include some of the parts listed above, but not all parts. A PPA must include the following:

- Postcard
- Payment
- Transmittal letter (Different than that required for a non-PPA)
- Fee transmittal

- Drawings

- Specification

The only sections of the specification that are required include the title, drawing figures, description, and operation of the main embodiment and the description and operation of any alternative embodiments.

Figure 4 - Patent Application Declaration Form

chapter twelve

Patent Application Processing

The PTO employs about 1,200 examiners to review patent applications and determine whether an invention is patentable. Patent examiners have technical expertise and training in such fields as engineering, chemistry, physics, and law. Completed, non-provisional patent applications are assigned to patent examining groups that have expertise in the area of technology related to the invention. An application is then assigned to a patent examiner for examination in the order in which it is received. An application will not be advanced out of turn, except as required by the rules of the PTO.

It may take years to process a patent application. The average time for the PTO to process a patent application is 32 months, but that average is calculated over thousands of applications. Dependent upon the complexity and scope of the application, the time may be longer or shorter.

Patent Applications

No patent will be issued from a provisional application. The application is never examined and kept secret by the PTO. A provisional application must be followed by a non-provisional application within one year or the provisional application is destroyed and never made public. A non-provisional patent application will be processed and examined by the PTO. The legal requirement for a patent application dictates that the application include a description of the preferred embodiment of the invention and at least one claim. To convince a PTO examiner to actually issue the patent, the application must clearly show utility, novelty and non-obviousness of the invention, as defined by the PTO.

Patent Application Examination

A patent examiner is responsible to review patent applications, conduct anticipating patent searches, and draft an examination report. The patent examiner will issue formal communication to the applicant, with supporting citations and court rulings, and expect that responses follow the same formal style. Responses should include contrary citations or rulings that support the position taken. An examination of a patent application consists of a study of the application for compliance with legal requirements of the particular type of patent, a patent search of U.S. patents, a search of foreign patent documents and a search of available literature. The study and searches are required to determine whether the invention meets the requirements for novelty and non-obviousness.

Patent Office Actions

The results of studies and searches conducted by the PTO are documented in a patent office "action" that is mailed to the attorney, agent, or person of record. An office action indicates whether claims of the invention are rejected, objected, or allowed. The action indicates any adverse action to be taken, any objection to the application, or any requirement that needs to be met. The action also indicates any information or references that may be useful to the applicant in deciding whether to move forward with patent application process. In examining a patent application, the patent examiner determines whether each claim of the invention is applicable to patentable subject matter and meets the requirements for novelty and non-obviousness. If so, the claim is accepted. If not, the claim is rejected. It is commonplace for claims to be rejected on the first office action by the patent examiner. Very few patents applications are filed as a result of the first application.

Response to Office Actions

In response to an office action, it is the responsibility of the patent applicant to request reconsideration of the patent application in writing. The request must specifically dispute each instance of objection or rejection documented in the patent examiner's office action. The request cannot simply indicate that the examiner was in error; the request must indicate an attempt to dispute the allegations so as to advance the application to a final action. The only exception is that the request is to objections or requirements as to form. Objections and requirements as to form have no bearing on further consideration of the claims. The applicant may request that such objections and requirements be held in abeyance until allowable subject matter is submitted.

In response to a rejection of claims, the applicant must submit an amended application that clearly specifies one or more of the following:

- That which makes the amended claims patentable despite any prior-art or objections referenced.

- How the amended claims avoid the state of referenced prior art or objections.

After submitting a response to the rejection, the application will be reconsidered and examined in light of the additional information provided by the applicant. The examiner will examine the initial application and any responses provided by the applicant. As with the first office action, a decision will be made as to whether to reject, object to, or accept the claims of the invention. In most instances, the second office action is made final.

Any response to an office action must be made within a specified time. Statute dictates that the maximum time period is six-months, but statute also provides the PTO with the authority to shorten the time period to no less than 30 days. The typical time established for responses is three months. When a shorter time is specified it may be up to the six-month maximum. An extension of time is usually granted at cost, the cost dependent on the length of the extension.

If no reply is received within the specified time, the application is considered abandoned and its pendency period is ended. However, the application may be revived if the applicant is able to prove that the failure to respond was unavoidable or unintentional. A revival must be petitioned from the PTO and requires that a fee be paid. Justification must accompany the petition, if no justification has been filed.

Patent Application Rejections

The patent examiner may issue a final office action that indicates a rejection of claims. In the final office action, the examiner repeats all grounds for rejection that are applicable to the claims of the application. If a second or later office action results in a final rejection, the applicant's response is limited to an appeal of the claim. Any further amendments to the application are subject to restrictions. A rejection of claims or a final rejection may be brought before the PTO's Board of Patent Appeals and Interferences. The applicant is required to pay a fee for the appeal and file a brief to support the position taken. An oral hearing will be held, if requested, upon payment of the required fee.

If the decision handed down by the board is adverse to the patent applicant, an appeal may be taken to the Court of Appeals for the Federal Circuit or a civil action may be filed against the PTO in the U.S. District Court for the District of Columbia. The Court of Appeals will review the record established at the PTO and affirm or reverse the decision of the office action. A civil action requires that the applicant present testimony to the court and the court will make a decision as to monetary damages.

As an alternative to an appeal to the Board of Patent Appeals and Interferences, an applicant may file application for a new continuation. A new continuation may be sought for consideration of different claims or consideration of further evidence. The new application requires that the applicant pay a filing fee and submit the claims or evidence for which consideration is being sought. If the application for continuum is filed before the expiration of the period for appeal and specific reference is made to the earlier filed application, the applicant will be entitled to the earliest filing date for all subject matter common to both the initial and continuation application.

Objection to Form

Petitions must be bought before the PTO for objections and requirements not involved in the rejection of claims. The applicant's response to a final rejection or office action may include either a cancellation of the rejected claim or appeal from the rejection of each claim. However, if any claim is allowed, the applicant must comply with requirements or objection as to the form of the claim. Applicants may arrange to hold an interview with the patent examiner, but an interview does not eliminate the necessity to respond to office actions within the specified period of time.

Claiming More Than One Invention

If more than one embodiment of an invention is claimed in

a single patent application and the PTO decides that a single patent is not sufficient to cover all of the inventions, the applicant will be required to restrict the application to one or number of inventions determined suitable by the PTO. The PTO charges a fee for filing a patent application, and that fee entitles the applicant to the examination of just one invention. If two claims of an invention are directed towards subject matter that is classified in two separate subclasses, the patent examiner may require the applicant to restrict the application to just one of the claims. Also, when a patent application contains both a method claim and an apparatus claim, the patent examiner may require the applicant to restrict the application to just one of the claims. Even if both claims are directed to the same invention, a patent examiner may consider them to be two separate inventions.

Divisional Patent Application

When the PTO imposes such restrictions on a patent application, the applicant may file a second application known as a divisional patent application. Divisional patent applications share the filing date of the earliest filed invention. Divisional applications require additional fees and they may be filed at any time before the patent for the original application issues. However, applicants are encouraged to file divisional applications as soon as possible because any patent that issues as a result of a divisional application will expire 20 years from the date of the originally filed application.

In a similar circumstance, claims of several embodiments or species of a single invention are included in a patent application. In the first office action from the patent examiner, the applicant may be required to restrict the application to claim one species for the purpose of examination and facilitating a search. However, if a generic claim is allowed, the applicant is allowed to claim a reasonable number of different species of the invention. If a generic claim is not allowed, the applicant will be allowed to claim only the elected species, and a divisional application will be required for each additional species.

To avoid restrictions and the necessity of filing divisional applications, applicants may include a linking claim to the patent application. A linking patent claim is a complex claim that includes features of two inventions. An invention, for example, that includes both a product and a process claim may include a linking chain that links the product made by and to the process. The complexity of linking chains may require the services of a patent professional to ensure that it is properly documented.

Amendments to the Patent Application

It may become necessary to amend a patent application in response to an office action or other request of a patent examiner. Amendments provided in response to a final rejection or final office action may serve to cancel claims or put the application in compliance with a requirement of form, but it will not relieve the application from a condition that is subject to appeal or save it from abandonment. An amendment does not serve as a matter of right for an appealed case, after an appeal decision is made. Amendments will only be accepted as established by rules. If an amendment is submitted after such time that would otherwise be inappropriate, such as following a final rejection or an appeal, the applicant must present good and sufficient reasons for the necessity of the late submission.

When requested by a patent examiner, an applicant must submit amendments to claims, specifications, and drawings. The amendment may be necessary to correct inaccuracies or the wordiness of the definitions and the description, or it may be necessary to correct relationships between the claims, the drawings, and/or the description. An amendment to substantiate drawings, claims, or specifications must not include new matter beyond that which was originally disclosed. New matter includes matter that is neither derived from or an addition to matter specified in the original disclosure. Even when new matter is supported by a supplemental oath or declaration, it cannot be added as part of an amendment. New matter must be shown and claimed in a separate patent application.

Amending a claim includes amending the language of particular claims, canceling particular claims, or presenting new claims. Amended claims are, in fact, new claims. Any new claims must specify how they avoid any reference or ground for rejection that is pertinent.

Patent rules insist that erasures, insertions, additions, or any other types of alterations not be made to documents submitted with a patent application. The applicant is required to submit an amendment to the patent application that requests that such changes or additions be made. If words are to be inserted or removed, the amendment must specify exactly where the modification is to occur. The PTO documents amendments by drawing a red ink line through the word or words to be deleted and inserting red ink characters for additions. Short additions are inserted at the exact point specified by the amendment, longer additions are indicated by reference.

Drawings may not be changed, except with the permission of the PTO. Changes in construction of the drawing require the substitution of a new drawing. The new drawing must be provided in permanent ink and indicate the proposed changes. For the new drawing to become part of the record for the patent, the applicant must make a separate request to amend the original drawing. The applicant must file the request for approval by the PTO before any new drawings are filed.

If amendments are rendered too difficult to consider because of the number or nature of amendments or if it becomes too cumbersome to arrange the papers for printing and copying, the applicant may be required to rewrite the specification or claims in part or in their entirety.

The original numbering of claims is to be preserved throughout the processing of a patent application. If claims are later cancelled, the remaining claims are not to be renumbered. If claims are added by amendment or substituted for cancelled claims,

IN THE UNITED STATES PATENT AND TRADEMARK OFFICE

Serial Number: _____

Appn. Filed: _____

Applicant(s): _____

Appn. Title _____

Examiner/GAU: _____

Mailed: _____

At: _____

Amendment _____

Commissioner for Patents

P.O. Box 1450

Alexandria, VA 22313-1450

Sir:

In response to the Office Letter mailed _____ ,20_____ ,please amend the above application as follows:

☐ SPECIFICATION: Amendments to the specification begin on page___ of this amendment.

☐ DRAWINGS: Amendments to the drawings are discussed on page___ of this amendment.

☐ CLAIMS: Amendments to the claims begin on page___of this amendment.

☐ REMARKS: begin on page___ of this amendment.

Figure 5 - Patent Application Declaration Form

their numbering must follow, in consecutive order, the highest numbered claim previously presented. When the application is ready for approval, the patent examiner will be responsible to reorder the claims in consecutive order or an order specified and requested by the applicant.

Corrections to Patents

Despite the thorough review and examination of patent applications, patents are sometimes issued in error. When a printed patent does not correspond to the record held by the PTO, the PTO may issue the applicant a certificate correcting any clerical error made on its behalf, typically typographical errors made in printing. If the applicant makes a clerical error that needs to be corrected, the PTO will charge a fee to issue a certificate of correction.

When an issued patent is determined to be defective, patent laws allow for the inventor or applicant to apply for a reissue patent. The law limits the nature of changes that may be made and no new matter may be added. A reissue patent is granted only to replace the original patent and the grant is extended only for the balance of the unexpired term. A reissue patent will not extend the life of a patent beyond that granted for the original patent.

Any patent may be reexamined upon request, based on the existence of prior art. Such prior art may include existing patents or existing printed publications. Reexamination proceedings are held and the results of the proceedings are issued to the requesting party. Any person may make request for a reexamination so long as required fees are paid.

Patent Markings

Patented articles that are sold by, for, or under the patent owner are required to be marked as patented articles using the word "Patent" and the patent number. The penalty for failure to mark patented articles properly is a loss of the right to sue an infringer unless the infringer was duly notified of the infringement and failed to cease the infringing actions after receiving such notice. Consequently, the marking of an article as patented when an article has not been patented is illegal. If a patent application has been filed but the patent is pending, it is acceptable to mark articles of sale with the terms "Patent Applied For," "Patent Pending," or some similar term or terms. These terms, however, have no legal basis. They are intended only to give notice that a patent has been filed with the PTO and is pending issuance. The protection provided by patents does not begin until the PTO issues a grant of patent.

Patent Publication

Utility and plant patent applications are published 18 months after the filing date. The applicant may, however file a Non-Publication Request form along with the patent application, requesting that the application not be published. A request for non-publication cannot be denied.

International Patents

With the invention of the Internet and the growth of global business practices, a U.S. patented invention is just as vulnerable to infringement in markets outside of the United States as it is in the United States. To protect a patent from infringement in other countries, it must be secured in those other countries. The cost of engaging such a plan of action could be substantial, and the costs should be weighed against the probability of generating additional revenue from licensing the patent in foreign nations.

U.S. inventors who wish to file foreign patent applications are likely to seek assistance from foreign patent agents who are familiar with the patent process in the countries where patents are sought. In most countries patent professionals are called agents rather than attorneys. Foreign agents, such as U.S. agents are licensed to represent inventors before the PTO but not in a court of law. Foreign patent agents may be located from a number of sources. Inventors are cautioned to seek references and background information regarding any potential foreign patent agent and require a written estimate of the projected and expected cost of services. Foreign patent agents may be located from the following sources:

- **Telephone directories.** The telephone directory of the particular city where the patent office is located may be used to find patent agents in the particular foreign nation.

- **Consulates.** Most foreign nations have consulates in major U.S. cities that may assist with locating patent agents in their particular country.

- **The Martindale-Hubbell Law Directory.** The Martindale-Hubbell Law Directory lists a select group of foreign patent attorneys in each foreign nation, **www.martindalehubbell.com**.

- **British or German firms of patent agents.** If an inventor seeks to file a patent application in Europe, a British firm of patent agents, or a German firm located in Munich may be hired to complete all EPO filings. Though the German professionals may not be as fluent in English, they offer the benefit of physical proximity to the EPO. The EPO lists registered patent agents and law firms at its Web site located at **www.european-patent-office.org/online**.

- **Internet searches.** The Internet may be used to locate suitable patent agents in foreign nations. Search tools may be used to search by country and other parameters of interest.

chapter thirteen

Marketing and Manufacturing a Patented Invention

The more developed an invention, the more profitable the invention in the marketplace. In general, a concept or idea is not marketable. However, a patented invention that is built around a product, process, or method and is protected by IP rights, acquires interest in the marketplace. A patented invention that represents an unproven product, process, or method may not be as attractive, but does offer the potential to be sold and licensed. A patented invention requires expert marketing and manufacturing strategies to gain recognition and interest in the marketplace. Companies that propose to have the capability to market anything to anybody should be avoided. Very few large companies and very few responsible companies respond to unsolicited offers or proposals for licensing. Experts offer the benefit of guarding against mistakes in a complicated market. In negotiating licensing or other aspects of a patented invention, companies are not likely to maintain confidentiality of a disclosed device or concept. The fine print of most manufacturers' non-disclosure agreements includes clauses that render any promise of confidentiality meaningless. Marketing should be directed to those manufacturers that are most likely to benefit from the invention. An inventor must be capable of acquiring product liability insurance to protect a patented invention that imposes risks of personal injury. The insurance need not only be acquired but also acquired at a reasonable cost. Experts in marketing and manufacturing have knowledge of these nuances and are capable of negotiating the most cost effective solutions.

Inventor's Manufacturing and Marketing Plan

There are many factors that an inventor needs to consider in developing a manufacturing and marketing plan. The market potential of an invention should include an evaluation of the invention against similar or competitive products and services.

Cost Considerations

The inventor needs to consider factors that will make the invention more or less expensive to build, sell, or implement than similar or competitor products or processes. The invention should offer profitability or high sales volume when it represents a commodity in the market where pricing standards have already been established.

Physical Characteristics

The inventor needs to establish whether the addition or reduction of size, durability, novelty, or weight offers any benefit over existent products. The size and weight of an invention will affect processing and the cost of packing and shipping. Durability is commonly interpreted as a positive asset, especially for high cost goods and products that fall in the "re-usable" goods market. However, the lack of durability has benefited other markets, such as the "disposable" goods market. The disposable battery has done well in the marketplace and continues to sustain growth, as many portable inventions are reliant upon their manufacture. Novelty and design will affect salability, particularly when the design also offers better functionality or an alternative over existing ways. If the invention involves viewing, such as with a TV screen or computer monitor, the technology must meet or exceed those standards already established for competitiveness. If the novelty of an invention is highly visible, the product may offer an advantage over products where the novelty is hidden. As an example, a pair of Velcro fastened shoes offers visible novelty whereas a pair of shoes equipped with comfort-designed insoles has its novelty hidden, particularly if the specially designed insoles are not implied by the brand.

Functionality

When an invention offers speed, ease of use, or convenience over similar or competitor products or services, the invention offers the advantage of improved functionality. Also, when the invention proves to be superior, offering a longer life cycle and better operability, the functionality, alone, may be used to market and promote the invention. In the fast paced world of technology, some inventions suffer anachronism by the time they are developed, manufactured, and brought to market. In the software market, for example, a well-devised invention could be developed to "fix" a glitch in a piece of software that is widely used and distributed. At the same time, another inventor could be developing a new piece of software that completely replaces the known software and also eliminates the software glitch. If both pieces of software, the "fix" and the new software, are marketed at the same time, the "fix" is likely to experience a much shorter life cycle than the newly revised software package.

Consumer Satisfaction

Consumer satisfaction is the primary factor affecting the sale of any new product or service. An invention may satisfy the consumer if the product or service is capable of offering the excitement of something that:

- Meets existing needs.

- Is compatible with or is an add-on to existing products or services.

- Offers a potentially long life cycle.

- Offers advancement over existing solutions.

- Requires a short learning curve.

- Is part of the current and latest fad.

If consumer satisfaction is met, the inventor may benefit from markups. However, if consumers feel burdened by the change because it is too radical, the invention may not do well. The government's insistence upon the use of the metric system suffered inertia despite claims that the system would be easier to understand. Rather than add simplicity in the weights and measures used for goods and products, the new system confused the consumer into demanding the old system of weights and measurements that was already known. If consumers are forced to endure a steep learning curve, acceptance may be long sought.

Operability

An invention is practical or operable if it is readily workable and does not require additional design or development. Issues of operability are usually apparent when the inventor attempts to build a working model of the invention. A working model should be established as soon as possible to test for any flaws and defects that may hamper operability, and thus, marketability. A great-looking design may create interest in an invention, initially, but if the invention is not readily operable, interest will not be sustained. Also inventions that require frequent servicing and adjustments offer a disadvantage, particularly when other similar inventions are readily available on the market that do not require such service or adjustments. If the invention presents a truly new concept or process, it may sustain itself in the market for as long as no improvement is competitively situated in the marketplace.

Ease of Production

Inventions that are easily produced and distributed are more easily marketed. Inventions that are large, fragile, or perishable require more costly or time-consuming methods of both production and distribution.

Environmental Issues

In our more environmentally conscious society, inventions that make use of waste products, reduce the use of limited natural resources, or produce few waste products offer an advantage. Inventions that eliminate noise and odor, convert noise into a more acceptable sound, and convert noise or odor to function as an alarm are advantageous in the marketplace. The latter is characterized by inventions such as smoke detectors and motion-sensor lighting.

Marketability

Inventions dependent upon other goods or services incur whatever growth or loss the goods or services experience in the market. Replacement parts, for example, are dependent on the sale and use of the parts, themselves. If the market for the part goes into a slump, sales of the replacement part will fall off, particularly when the replacement part serves no other useful purpose. Inventions that present a liability risk, such as drugs, firearms, contact sports, safety devices, or motorized vehicles, may suffer from consumer concerns. Inventions likely to be the subject of lawsuits against the manufacturer due to malfunction, safety, or health risks are much harder to market to investors. To secure investments in these types of inventions, investors will need to be convinced that the invention has a potential to sell. Obsolete inventions are also not likely to offer a return on investment dollars. Inventions that are so technically advanced that they or their use is not understood may suffer inertia during the life of the patent that protects them. The computer mouse, for example, was patented and the patent expired in 1980, just before the product became most popular. An inventor should ensure that the invention is marketable during the life of the patent. Inventions that are most easy to promote are most easily marketable. Inventions that are difficult or expensive to promote or require a long time to promote are at a disadvantage. These inventions include such things as new technology and bulky, awkward or expensive goods or services. If an invention has no existing market, the inventor can expect to expend a large amount of money on promotion and convincing the public that it needs the particular invention. Having a prototype available to demonstrate a tangible product or service is an advantage. Establishing the broadest possible coverage for an invention offers the inventor a monopoly in the marketplace.

Development

A fully developed invention should be ready to market. If such things as design issues, which may include market appearance, material selection, or specialized packaging have not been resolved, delays will be necessary to incorporate additional engineering for the invention.

Production Facilities

Each new invention requires a new or modified production facility, which means incorporating appropriate tooling and production techniques that are unique to the invention. In the rare instance that an invention requires no change in an existing production facility or the invention requires only a modest change, the invention offers an advantage.

Combination Products

Products that are composed of a combination of more than one invention are hard to market when the two inventions do not work in unison. The clock radio is a novel invention that continues to enjoy success. The telephone-clock-radio, however, did not prove to be as successful. The addition of the telephone did not offer the anticipated unison or functionality. In addition, the concept was outdated by the invention of the cordless phone.

Inventor's Decision Analysis

There are several scenarios that determine to whom and at what point it is best to sell an invention. In many instances it may be more advantageous for the inventor to market, distribute and sell an invention on his or her own. In other instances, it may be more advantageous to sell the invention or rights to the invention and allow another party to handle the marketing and manufacturing processes.

An inventor may want to consider selling an invention to a manufacturer before a non-provisional patent application has been filed. If an inventor has filed a provisional patent application (PPA) or built and tested the invention and properly recorded those activities, selling to manufacturer offers the benefit of allowing the manufacturer to prepare the permanent patent application either on the basis of the PPA or without the PPA. However, if an inventor fails to document and record building and testing activities properly, the inventor risks having the manufacturer steal the invention by filing for a patent. Also, if a PPA is not properly filed, it may lead to delays in obtaining a non-provisional patent, hindrance to obtaining foreign patents and hindrance to licensing the invention.

An inventor may file for a patent and then sell rights to the invention. This is the most common method of profiting from an invention since most inventors are not capable of establishing a manufacturing and distribution facility to complement the invention. Even if a patent search indicates that an invention is not patentable because it closely resembles prior art, the invention may still be profitable and sold to a manufacturer. If the invention offers significant novelty it may be cleverly marketed and protected by one of the other IP rights, such as trademark. As an example, Kodak film does not offer significant novelty to be protected under a utility patent, but the yellow film packaging allows it to be protected under trademark laws with a design patent.

In many cases it is a hard sell to get manufacturers to back an invention that doesn't offer the potential for patentability under a utility patent and thus, market position. If the invention is unique and serves a useful purpose, the inventor may be more successful in making and distributing the invention on his or her own rather than trying to sell the invention to a manufacturer. The inventor would be privy to market advantage rather than the menial return that would be offered if, by chance, a manufacturer did decide to buy into it.

In contrast, there are also inventions that are commercially valuable and patentable but are best not patented. Instead it would be more profitable to maintain a trade secret and use the secret in business to give a business a competitive edge. A special formula, for example, may be held as a trade secret for years as long as persons with access to it maintain the secrecy of the invention. If, however, the same invention were patented, patent laws would require public disclosure of the formula and invite others to copy or manipulate the formula.

If the trade secret protection route does not prove to offer advantages, the inventor may always file a patent application and continue to manufacture and distribute the invention with a "patent pending" notice. However, manufacturing and marketing a patentable invention is not recommended because it opens the door for patent rights to be lost or for the invention to be stolen. The "one year rule" dictates that a patent application must be filed within one year of marketing or disclosing the invention in the United States, or patent rights are lost, and most foreign countries insist upon novelty or patent rights are lost if the invention is disclosed before application for a patent is made. Also, since the patent application is publicly disclosed 18 months after making application, another party may copy the invention and fraudulently file a patent application for the invention.

If an inventor does decide to market an invention before filing for a patent, it is recommended that the inventor give the invention about a nine-month period on the market to determine its commercial success. If it is successful, the inventor should begin to file application for a patent immediately to avoid pitfalls of the one-year rule. If the invention is not successful, the inventor should consider dropping it. However, inventors are expected to be realistic and use good judgment in following these guidelines to determine whether to file for a patent application.

Selling an Invention

The primary reason for developing an invention is to sell it and make a profit. To sell an invention, the inventor must be capable of publicizing and advertising the invention to potential buyers. While there are advantages to selling a patented invention, an inventor need not wait for a patent before introducing the invention to potential buyers or potential licensees. In fact, inventors are encouraged to sell or license their inventions as soon as possible after filing application for a patent because it gives potential buyers a head start on competition, time to get the patent in force and have the patent issuance coincide with the time the invention is put on the market. It also gives a manufacturer an opportunity to apply for foreign patent rights before the patent issues. If an inventor is able to provide prospective buyers with a favorable search report that indicates no threatening prior art exists, the report serves as proof that the invention is patentable.

An invention, patented or not, is worthless if it cannot be commercially exploited. Many inventions have been patented that have never yielded a profit. In order to sell or license an invention, the invention must be marketable and then marketed. To develop, market, and sell an invention takes time. However, the market for inventions is neither rational nor linear. Dependent upon marketing and promotional techniques, it is possible for an inferior invention to be successful and a superior invention to fail in the marketplace.

Marketing and Manufacture

Many inventors outsource the services of others to take on the difficult tasks of marketing and manufacturing their invention. The inventor is then provided more time to sell the invention or the patent for the invention. Several companies exist to market inventions on a contingent-fee basis. Inventors are encouraged to check with friends, associates, inventors' organizations, colleges, or universities with invention marketing departments and to search the Internet to locate potential intermediaries. There are seven primary and differing ways of getting an invention to market. They include the following:

Using an Intermediary

An intermediary, also referred to as a contingent-fee broker, invention developer, invention marketer, or invention promoter, is a firm that represents an inventor in marketing the invention for the purpose of selling or licensing it for a percentage of the inventor's rights. There are two categories of intermediaries, contingent-fee brokers and fee-based inventor-exploiters (FBIEs). A contingent-fee broker differs from a FBIE since contingent-fee brokers do not charge the inventor fees for their services but expect a fair and reasonable form of compensation for services completed. FBIEs charge inventors a fee for their services, and they are more likely to profit from fees acquired from inventors than the sale or license of the invention.

Intermediaries offer the benefit of doing the legwork to seek manufacturers and present an invention to them. The disadvantage of hiring intermediaries is that they are not likely to share the same enthusiasm for an invention that the inventor has. Also, the inventor must establish a method of verifying the efficiency of a chosen intermediary and ensuring that any contractual agreement is adhered to. Inventors may check an intermediary's reputation and sense of integrity by consulting with patent attorneys or inventor organizations and any supplied references. Intermediaries may perform a number of duties and the language of any contract should clearly indicate which set of duties the intermediary will perform. Some common duties include the following:

- Identifying potential manufacturers.
- Preparing a presentation for the invention.
- Preparing a demonstration of the invention.
- Building and testing the invention.
- Submitting the invention to prospects.
- Negotiating a license or sales agreement.

Most importantly, the language of the contract should specify a time for completing all specified duties and accomplishing the task. If, for example, the intermediary is hired to get the invention on the market in product form, a time limit should be established for completing this task and it should be specified in the contract agreement. Further, the language of the contract should specify if the intermediary fails to complete the task in the specified time, all rights are to be returned to the inventor along with all presentations, research, documents, and models.

Partial Use of an Intermediary

Though this practice is seldom used, an inventor may hire the services of an intermediary only for the purpose of locating prospects in the market. After prospects are identified, the inventor takes on the job of promoting and selling the invention. Most contingent-fee brokers will not accept this type of arrangement because they want to exercise control over the final sales negotiations with the manufacturer. However, inventor assistance companies will provide inventors with product evaluations, advertising, market research, illustrations, packaging design, and product testing services for a fee.

Seek a Manufacturer and Distributor

The inventor who chooses to find a manufacturer and distributor for an invention must engage in the necessary research to locate a suitable candidate and then be capable of selling the idea of manufacturing or marketing the invention. When an inventor finds his own manufacturer and distributor, the inventor is not obligated to share any portion of the rights to the invention, as would be the case if the services of an intermediary were used. Most independent inventors prefer to do their own market research and selling because it offers the advantage of 100 percent of the rewards. The inventor controls the manufacturing and distribution process without having to manufacture and distribute the invention.

The Working Model

The best method of selling an invention to a manufacturer is to demonstrate a working model or prototype of the invention. Visual aides, such as pictures, graphs, and diagrams may be useful in describing the technical and functional aspects of an invention, but a working model or prototype indicates that the invention is real and doable. A model made of wood or cardboard is more effective than no model at all. The model or prototype should be presented in simplicity because simplicity has the effect of enhancing reliability, reducing costs and weight, and facilitating salability.

Often an inventor will have to acquire the services of a model maker to build the working model. Model makers are specially trained experts who may be sought through invention organizations, inventor magazines, the yellow pages, machine shops, colleges, universities, local industry, and Internet searches. When acquiring a model maker, the inventor may have to disclose sensitive information about the invention, which should be protected by a Consultant's Work Agreement before such proprietary information is disclosed. Any drawings, descriptions, or other documentation provided to a model maker should be marked with a confidentiality legend. Such a legend may be attached to documents in type, with a sticker or a stamp.

At least one professional quality photograph should be taken of the working model, but more than one is recommended, preferably showing various views. Each photograph should then be duplicated with at least 50 glossy prints and attached to paper, preferably with multiple views on a single sheet. To complement the photographs, a descriptive narrative of the invention should be documented. The narrative should be short, concise, and to the point. The narrative should include a title or trademark, the inventor's name address and telephone number. It should describe what the invention is, how the invention works, its advantages and its selling points. A legend indicating, "Patent Pending," should also be included on the sheet. The narrative should then be printed and duplicated with at least 50 copies.

If a real working model cannot be made, a virtual prototype may be computer-generated. An inventor may have to engage the services of a graphic artist with simulation or computer aided design (CAD) expertise to create this type of model or prototype.

Criteria for Potential Manufacturers

The inventor must compile a list of potential manufacturers thought to be capable of manufacturing and distributing the invention profitably. Potential manufacturers should meet the following criteria.

- **Experience manufacturing the same or closely related products.** A company that has past experience with the same or similar product is more likely to be aware of competitive pricing policies and know how to sell in the particular field of the invention. They are more likely to be capable of adding a new invention to an existing product line, keeping sales costs low.

- **Enthusiastic about bringing new products to market.** Manufacturers who have experience with a similar product or are closely allied with the particular product are more likely to want to add a new product to their existing product line to keep ahead of competition.

- **Geographically close to the inventor.** When a manufacturer is local or nearby, the inventor may more easily monitor progress, consult with the producers more frequently, and take any required actions that may be necessary.

- **Not too large.** Smaller manufacturers offer many benefits to the inventor. Smaller companies are more reliant on outside designers for inventions than on inventions that they themselves have created, and a smaller company is less likely to request that the inventor release certain legal rights by signing of a waiver. When the bureaucracy is small, it allows for more rapid decision-making, and it is likely to provide more direct contact with top management or owners. Smaller companies are not likely to have funds to maintain access to patent attorneys. As such, they are less likely to try and get around manufacturing the invention by investigating the potential to invalidate the patent or avoid infringing upon it. Smaller companies will be more concentrated on the profit potential of the invention and its effect on the marketplace. On the other hand, inventors should not engage the services of companies that are so small that they will not have the funds to finance the manufacture and market of the invention. Companies with sales in the range of $10 million to $100 million dollars are recommended unless, of course, the invention has enormous market potential. If in this case, it may be more advantageous to seek the services of a larger corporation.

There are numerous sources that may assist an inventor in finding a suitable company that meets the criteria to manufacture an invention. Friends and associates are always a good source of information. The inventor should also check out local stores for similar or closely allied products and determine the manufacturer of those products. If products already exist on the shelf, the manufacturer obviously has a successful distribution and sales operation. Inventor's magazines, such as *Inventor's Digest* or *The Patent Café*, run advertisements and may have listings of companies seeking new products from inventors. Inventors must research and evaluate such companies because some may be scams. The library may also have registers, directories, and other resources that list local and national manufacturers. Some suggested resources include the California Manufacturers Register, the Thomas Register, and Dun's Million Dollar Directory. Also trade magazines, hobby magazines, and stock advisory services, such as Moody's, Standard & Poor's and Value Line Investment Survey, provide information about companies.

If an invention falls into the category of gadgets and the inventor would like to appeal to a more affluent group of consumers, the Hammacher Schlemmer specialty store and mail order house in New York and the Sharper Image Products Committee in California develop and sell a wide variety of gadgets both over-the-counter and through their catalogs. Each of these of these companies receives and accepts new inventions and then arranges to have them produced by manufacturers. Many products are financed, manufactured, or first sold under these companies and have transitioned from luxury items to common household products. The following products that are commonplace in many households are evidence of such a transition.

Steam iron	Pressure cooker	Humidifier
Electric razor	Electric can opener	Blender
Microwave oven	Automatic-drip coffee maker	High intensity lamp
Electrostatic air purifier	Non-fogging shower mirror	

Another company that may accept new inventions is JS&A. However, they will not be responsible for developing or manufacturing the invention but will sell the invention. Here are other U.S. companies that may assist with manufacturing a new invention.

Company	Type of Invention
Lisle Corporation, Indiana	New automotive tools
The Sharper Image, California	Executive gadgets
Homax Products	Home improvement products
Kraco Enterprises, Inc., California	New automotive products
Hog Wild Toys, Oregon	Novel toys and gifts
The Bohning Company, LTD, MI	New plastic products
NordicTrack, MN	New exercise or fitness equipment

Other prospective manufacturers may be sought at trade shows and trade fairs.

While most U.S. inventors will seek U.S. manufacturers, inventors are encouraged to seek foreign manufactures if a U.S. manufacturer cannot be located. It must be noted that some U.S. companies may not undertake new inventions that have received acceptance from foreign companies. With the proper strategy, an inventor may use this to his or her advantage.

The Invention Presentation

Before an inventor presents a demonstration of the invention to a manufacturer, the inventor must research the stability and competence of the chosen company. Larger corporations, with corporate engineering departments already in place for the purpose of developing new inventions for the company, may be biased toward inventions created in-house. If an outside inventor is able to produce an invention that is a logical extension of ideas already in development within the company, the company may be more receptive of the invention. Because of the uncertainty in a company's response to a new idea, inventors are sometimes reluctant to present their inventions to companies, even after filing application for a patent, because it seems logical that a company with its vast resources may have an interest in stealing the invention rather than paying for it. However, if the invention is properly recorded with a built and tested working model (if applicable) and a properly submitted patent application, most companies wouldn't want to risk being sued for infringement.

The In-Person Presentation

A brief, friendly, sincere letter should be sent to the president of a potential manufacturer. The letter should indicate that the invention is of value and profit to the company's business. The letter should request an appointment to provide a brief demonstration of the invention. A brief and general disclosure of the invention is recommended, but the real essence of the invention should not be disclosed until the demonstration takes place. The letter should also indicate that the inventor would be calling in a few days to follow up on the requests of the letter.

The demonstration should be well-prepared. The inventor should explain the advantages of the invention, how it works, how it will profit the company and why it will sell. The inventor should prepare written materials and photos for the company's management team and decision makers. Collectively, the presentation and supporting documents should cover form, fit, and function of the invention. Form describes the appearance of the invention and should stress its attractiveness or its potential to be attractive. Fit describes how the invention fits with other products, fits the environment for which it is intended, or fits the future goals of the business. Function describes what and how the invention does what it does to achieve a result. The model or prototype should work, and the inventor should be prepared to answer any questions regarding functionality or processes.

Presentation via Correspondence

Though an in-person presentation is most suitable method of presenting an invention to potential manufacturers, it is possible to present an invention via correspondence. The correspondence should be inclusive of a sales letter addressed to a specific individual of the company, preferably the president. If a response indicating interest is received, the inventor should strive to coordinate an in-person presentation. If it is not possible, the inventor should be sure to get an advance written commitment from the company indicating that they will return any model or prototype that may be sent with the correspondence. The model should be delivered by certificated mail with a return receipt requested. The inventor must be sure to follow up with the company until any requested materials are returned. The Internet, e-mail, and online conferencing offer an alternative to paper communications. Documents and the working model may be electronically stored and delivered. However, the inventor must keep in mind that such transference of electronic information is permanent and any confidential information becomes vulnerable to the nuances of online and electronic theft.

Waiving Rights to the Invention

Companies, particularly large companies with readily available legal resources, will require an inventor to sign a waiver that relinquishes a number of important rights to the invention. Waivers are designed to protect companies from suits that may arise; claiming that the company violated some implied confidentiality agreement or violated an implied agreement to pay for the use of the invention or some specific part of the invention. In the past, many companies have lost these types of lawsuits, not so much because of the terms of the agreement, but because of the time, expense, resources, and uncertainty of litigation. Even in situations where the company's own inventors were responsible to develop an invention, independent of any outside inventor, companies have lost these types of lawsuits or settled for a compromise rather than deal with uncertainty and high cost of litigation.

A waiver requires that the inventor give up rights, but it may not force the inventor to relinquish any rights under patent laws. A typical waiver will require the inventor to agree that the company is not obligated to pay for use of an idea, to keep the idea of the invention confidential, to return any documents submitted and to have no obligation to the inventor except as established by patent laws. Many companies also add other minor provisions. In essence, a waiver relinquishes all rights against the company except to sue for patent infringement if and when a patent is acquired.

The usual procedure for most large companies is for the inventor to send correspondence to the company that introduces the invention or idea. The company usually forwards the correspondence to an appropriate individual in its patent or legal department. The patent or legal department will respond to the inventor by delivering a form letter, which details the company policy and requests that the inventor provide signature to a waiver before the company agrees to review the invention. Upon providing signature to the waiver, the invention submission is forwarded to the company's engineering department.

There are several issues with this process as follows:

- The patent, if not already issued, may not be issued.

- The company may use a variation of the invention that may be covered by the issued patent.

- The company is not bound to keep the invention confidential.

It is because of these issues that an inventor should avoid large companies and waivers and concentrate on smaller companies that do not require a waiver. In fact, it is more advantageous for inventors to seek companies that are willing to sign an agreement that is drafted by the inventor. An agreement drafted by the inventor is known as a Proprietary Submission Agreement.

If an inventor is required to sign a waiver, the pending or acquired patent is still protected under patent laws with regards to first rights. The inventor must be sure to choose a reliable and fair company and insist that a decision be made within a reasonable time, usually six months, or return all documents to the inventor. Without an agreement with regard to making a decision, a company may takes years to make a decision which may interfere with other efforts to market the invention.

The Proprietary Submission Statement

A Proprietary Submission Statement is an agreement that stipulates that a company will agree to review an invention, keep the invention and all attached documents in confidence, to return all documents submitted, and to pay a reasonable sum and royalty if the invention is adopted. The requirement to pay reasonable fees and royalties should include language that specifies that the amounts of such funds be settled in the future through negotiation or arbitration. If a company refuses to provide signage, the Proprietary Submission Statement may be modified to eliminate the requirement for payment of fees and royalty or eliminate the requirement to keep all information confidential and allow the company to disclose any supplied information that exists as prior art that is or becomes part of the public domain invention. If these modifications still do not result in signed contract with a company, the inventor may have to rely solely upon having the company review the invention without a contract and settle for reasonably strong rights and protection as they apply under patent laws.

Selling the Invention

When an inventor sells an invention to a manufacturer or distributor, a contract agreement must be signed. The contract should clearly specify what is being sold and for how much.

Outsource the Manufacture and Distribution

Inventors may have an invention manufactured, usually by a far cheaper Far-Eastern manufacturer and then have a U.S. distributor sell the invention. The inventor benefits from the low cost of manufacture and relatively high costs of goods sold in the United States. The inventor will have to be responsible for supervising outsourced manufacturing operations, such as quality control and import/export procedures to assure that all processes and procedures fall within applicable laws and regulations.

Inventor as Distributor

Inventors may choose to engage a low-cost manufacturer and distribute the product on his or her own. The inventor has to supervise the manufacturing operation and perform more work but receives more profits.

Inventor as Manufacturer

Inventors may choose to engage in manufacturing the product on his or her own and allow another party to distribute the product.

Inventor as Manufacturer and Distributor

In this situation, the inventor performs all of the tasks and receives all of the profits. If an inventor intends to manufacture or market his own invention, the inventor must either establish a start-up company or make use of his or her existing company. In either case, marketing, manufacturing, and distribution of a newly established invention will require a plan to market and manufacture the invention as well as financial backing and publicity.

Marketing a patented invention should include the following:

- Identifying marketing and licensing opportunities.
- Identifying barriers to market entry.
- Developing a marketing plan.
- Developing a market description.

    Manufacturing a patented invention offers challenges since mistakes, such as the wrong process or materials, may cause the product or service to be rejected by manufacturers.

The inventor must decide whether he or she will take responsibility for marketing and manufacturing the invention or allow an outside party to handle the marketing and manufacturing processes.

Financing

If an inventor is planning to manufacture an unsold and untried product, traditional bankers are not likely to lend money to finance the operation. The inventor will need to seek funds as provided through a venture capitalist. A venture capitalist (VC) will lend money for such untried and unsold products in return for a portion of the company. VCs do not lend money on the same terms that are offered by traditional bankers. A VC's return on an investment is never fixed. The higher the risk involved, the more share and control a VC seeks in a company.

A more recent development in the field of VC is the creation of the Incubator VC. State and federal governments, private organizations, and academia sponsor Incubator VCs. Incubator VCs provide multiple inventors with manufacturing areas, labs, and office areas in a single building, which is referred to as an innovation center. The VC may also provide inventors with technical, marketing, financial and other forms of expertise to help nurture the business entity until it is capable of operating on its own.

For an inventor to acquire venture capital to establish a business around an invention, the inventor must prepare and provide the potential VC with a business plan. The business plan must detail the invention, the inventor's plan to market the invention, and a planned use for any acquired venture capital.

Publicity

At some point prior to production or immediately after

production of the invention has begun, the inventor will need to publicize the invention. There are several mediums available to the inventor to publicize his or her own invention, but the inventor must be diligent in meeting the requirements for publication. The inventor may engage in media publicity, public exhibitions, premium marketing, or celebrity endorsements. Other publicity ideas may be found in books, journals, trade magazines, periodicals, and other references or research publications in the field of the invention.

Professional Promoters

An inventor may hire the services of a public relations firm or marketing research firm to promote the invention. These professionals devise very valuable and creative methods to publicize an invention, but their services are extremely costly.

Media Promotion

Certain media outlets provide free publicity for new and interesting inventions. Radio shows, TV shows, newspapers, and magazines offer free publicity. Local radio and TV shows seek interesting guests and some may even offer inventors an opportunity to demonstrate or discuss their inventions. An inventor would need to seek out appropriate shows and make contact with the producer by sending a press kit or letter indicating how and why the invention would be of interest to the listening audience. Many magazines feature new inventions and ideas; some may also include a feature article of the new invention or idea if the invention holds the interest of the editor. Magazines that feature new inventions and ideas include the following:

• Apartment Life	• Argosy	• Better Homes and Gardens
• Changing Times	• House and Garden	• House Beautiful
• Jet	• McCall's	• Mechanics Illustrated

• Outdoor Life	• Outdoor Living	• Parade
• Playboy	• Popular Science	• Sunset
• This Week	• True Story	• Advertising Age

Exhibitions

Exhibits, trade shows, and business shows offer an opportunity to publicize an invention and also provide a hands-on demonstration of the inventions' techniques and capabilities. Thousands of these types of exhibitions are held throughout the country each year. The inventor must seek out those exhibitions that are appropriate for the type of invention being presented and make arrangements to present the invention attractively. These types of exhibitions and showings are relatively inexpensive, in the range of a couple hundred dollars. In most cases, the inventor is provided a booth or space to showcase the invention. A working model of the invention should be displayed such that it is attractive and interesting to the audience. The inventor should also use the opportunity to provide the audience with literature that promotes the invention. One of the disadvantages of this type of promotion is that others will have an opportunity to copy the invention in hopes of selling the invention or avoiding its patents. Sponsorship at a sporting event or other public function is also a relatively inexpensive method of showcasing an invention and acquiring publicity.

Celebrity Endorsements

When an inventor is capable of getting a celebrity to endorse an invention, the invention immediately attracts public attention. To get celebrity endorsements an inventor should perfect the invention, prepare sales and promotional materials for the invention and then approach the chosen celebrity. A celebrity endorsement means that the inventor will lose a significant share of the profits from an invention, but the loss may be offset by sales that are likely to surpass those acquired through other types of promotions.

Distribution

There are two primary methods of distributing an invention. There are magazine, media, and direct mail advertising. The United States has about 15,000 mail order houses that rely upon the novelty of both small and large suppliers. Most of their products come from small companies and they are constantly seeking new products. Many mail order distributors require a production sample and they will use the sample to decide whether the product is capable of meeting their demand. They develop their own ads as well as manufacture and distribute their own catalogs. They may purchase products in agreed upon quantities or they may take products on consignment.

If the invention is of use to the federal government, the inventor should contact the General Services Administration (GSA) to offer the product. The GSA will respond by sending an inventor the appropriate forms and instructions to be submitted. If it is an energy related invention that is deemed favorable by the National Bureau of Standards, the Department of Energy may provide inventors with a research grant to further the invention. Also, for inventions that may be of use to state and local governments, the inventor should make contact with appropriate procurement offices.

chapter fourteen

Protecting a Patent

A patent owner may sue any manufacturer who makes, offers for sale, sells, uses, or imports a patented device or practices a patented process covered by claims. A patent owner may also file suit against a retailer or the purchaser of a patented invention.

The theory of vicarious liability provides that a business be liable for infringement by its employees or agents under the following conditions:

- The agent acts under the direction or authority of the business entity.

- The employee acts within the scope of his or her employment.

- The business benefits from, approves of, or adopts the infringing activity.

The standard of successor liability provides that a business that makes purchase of another business entity be liable for any infringement committed by the purchased business under the following conditions:

- There exists an agreement between the businesses and the purchaser for the purchaser to assume liability.

- The two businesses form a merger.

- The purchaser is a continuation of the purchased business.

- The sale is fraudulent and engaged for the purpose of escaping liability.

Patents provide protection for an invention for as long as certain requirements are met. If those requirements are not met, patent rights may be lost. The PTO may issue a patent for an invention. However, the patent may not provide broad enough coverage to adequately protect the invention that is being challenged. The following situations create cause for the loss of patent rights.

- Failure to pay required maintenance fees for the patent.

- It is determined that the patent fails to describe the invention adequately.

- It is determined that the patent fails to define how to make or use the invention adequately.

- It is determined that the patent includes inadequate claims.

- The discovery of prior-art references indicates that the patent is not novel or is obvious.

- The patent owner engages in illegal conduct connected with the patent.

- Failure to disclose information or material to the PTO that constitutes fraud.

Infringement

Infringement in the United States occurs when a party other than the party who holds patent rights to an invention intentionally sells, makes, offers for sale, or uses a patented invention in the United States, any U.S. territory or any U.S. possession or the party imports the invention into the United States, during the term of the patent. Infringement also occurs if all the parts of a patented invention are created and shipped to a foreign nation with instructions for the assembly of such parts. A patented invention may also be infringed in outer space if the invention is made, used, or sold in outer space on a "space object" that is under the jurisdiction or control of the United States. Infringement can only occur during the life of a patent. As such, a patent must actually be issued for infringement to occur. Infringement cannot be argued during the pendency period of a patent application unless the patent application is published before the patent is issued. The patent owner may sue for royalties from the date of publication, provided a patent is later issued and the infringer has actual notice of the published application. The patent owner must mark patented devices with the patent number assigned by the PTO. If a patent owner fails to provide such a marking, damages may only be recovered from the date on which the infringing party was notified of the infringement.

Essential to defining infringement is the necessity of the infringement to occur without the consent of the patent owner. A patent owner may authorize the use of a patented invention. However, any attempt to extend that authorized use beyond that for which it was intended is a form of infringement. A patent owner, for example, may authorize a company to build and make use of a single patented device. Instead of making a single device, the company decides to build and use three such devices. The building of the additional devices constitutes an infringement. It does not matter whether the infringing party intentionally or inadvertently develops a patented invention; the unauthorized sale, use, or manufacture of the invention is infringement. The intent and knowledge of the infringer have no bearing on the act of infringement but may be used in determining the amount of monetary damages and the level of contribution to an infringing act.

Infringing Patent Claims

To qualify as infringement, a device or process must physically perform or posses all of the elements documented in at least one of the claims specified for a patented invention or the infringing device or process must meet requirements specified in The Doctrine of Equivalents. Each claim of a patented invention should define a different and distinct area of protected technology. An infringing device or process need not infringe on all of the claims of a patented invention, if it infringes on all of the elements in a single claim, it is infringement. If a claim includes four elements, a process or device must contain all four elements of the claim to infringe on the patented invention. If the process or device includes three or fewer elements of the claim, no infringement occurs. If an invention is supported by a dependent claim, a device or process must infringe upon the associated independent claim for infringement to occur. Dependent claims will not be considered infringed upon if the independent claim is not infringed. Also, the violating party does not have to make use of the totality of the patented invention. If the violator infringes on the essential parts of the patented invention, the violator may be guilty of infringement. When a device or process infringes on at least one claim in its entirety it is considered a direct infringement. When someone persuades another party to infringe or contributes to the infringement of another, it is considered indirect infringement.

Direct Infringement

A party commits a form of direct infringement, termed literal infringement, when he or she directly makes, uses, or sells a process or device, which contains every element of a patent claim. With literal infringement, the infringing process or device is a mere imitator of the patented process or device. In many instances, the infringing party attempts to capitalize on the success of a patented invention by capturing a market share of the proceeds from sales.

A party commits a form of direct infringement, termed equivalent infringement or infringement under the doctrine of equivalents, when he or she designs a process or device around a patent claim such that it functions in substantially the same manner and provides the same result as that of the patent claim.

Infringement under the Doctrine of Equivalents

The Doctrine of Equivalents is a judge-made rule that establishes infringement based upon the similarity of function, method, or results. The use of the doctrine has been met with controversy, and its application has been curtailed by virtue of a decision handed down by the Court of Appeals for the Federal Circuit. If an infringing device or process fails to match the patented invention's claims literally and the difference in devices is insubstantial relative to the functioning of the device or process, but the similarity of function, method, or results is substantial, a patent owner may establish infringement. For example, an element of a patent claim specifies a handset connected to a base unit. An accused device specifies and includes the use of a cellular phone. The traditional telephone unit literally fails to match a cellular phone. The difference in devices is insubstantial to the function of the invention because the invention would work no matter which device was used. The devices serve the same function and offer the same result. The doctrine excuses the differences and the accused device is considered an infringing device.

The Doctrine of Equivalents requires that every element of a claim be literally or equivalently present in the infringing device or process. Equivalents are elements of a device or steps of a process which were either available when the patent was issued or available after the patent was issued, but before the patent was infringed upon. The doctrine prevents an infringer from designing around patent claims by making minor alterations or using later developments that were not available when the patent application was filed. An element of little or no importance to the claims of an invention can have a wide range of equivalent elements, which are not disclosed in the specification of the patent application.

When a patent claim specially describes a function of an element rather than the structure of the element, the claim consists of a means-plus-function clause. In other words, a means-plus-function exists when a claim specifies a particular way to perform a function without describing how to perform the function or with what to perform the function. When the scope of a claim includes language that considers "means-plus-function," the means of performing the function is considered to be as described in the specification and its equivalents. The clause usually begins with the term "means." A hinge, for example, may be disclosed in a patent claim as, "a means of attaching a door to a cabinet," without indicating the type of device necessary to do so.

In a literal infringement case, the court would have to determine equivalency or whether the means described in the specification for the patented invention was the same or equivalent to the means of the infringing device. The specification or its equivalents may describe the means as that of a hinge. The means, however, may include any flexible linking device that may act as a hinge. Even when the infringing device is not a literal copy of the patented invention, infringement may still occur if the device or process performs substantially the same function, in substantially the same manner, and obtains the same result as the patented invention. The existence of the term "means" in a claim will not always be grounds for an equivalence analysis. If the means of a clause is specific and the infringing device meets the means clause, the mean-plus-function equivalency is unnecessary.

If the means of an invention discloses a physical structure that is insignificant to the claimed invention, many more equivalent structures may exist than would be the case if the characteristics of the structure were critical in performing the claimed function. As an example, if screws were the preferred embodiment and means of holding a cabinet together, then nails, dowels or other types of joints would constitute equivalent elements since the screws are not critical to the functioning of the cabinet.

An equivalent structure or act cannot embrace technology developed after a patent is issued. The comparison between what is disclosed in the patent specification and what is proposed as an equivalent must consider the overall structure or process. The infringing device or process may have fewer or more parts or fewer or more methods, but it functions in substantially the same way as the patented device or process.

If an element of a patent claim is amended during the patent application process, the claim is presumed narrowed so as to bar the doctrine of equivalents. The presumption can be challenged if the patent owner is able to demonstrate that the amendment involved a feature of the invention that was unforeseeable at the time of application or for some other reason could not be included in the original claim. In other words, the doctrine of equivalents may still apply in an infringement lawsuit when a claim has been amended provided the patent owner is able to overcome the presumption of the claim.

Indirect Infringement

Indirect infringement occurs by contributing to an infringement or persuading another party to engage in infringement. An indirect infringement cannot occur unless a direct infringement occurs. There are two ways to infringe indirectly upon a patent.

1. **Inducing Infringement.** A party is persuaded to make, use or sell a patented invention without authorization.

2. **Contributory Infringement.** A material component of an invention is sold with the knowledge that the component is designed for unauthorized use.

A party who sells infringing parts of an invention has not engaged in the act of infringement until or unless those parts are used in an infringing invention. A typical example includes a manufacturer that knowingly sells a patented device that serves no other use except as it is patented. When a buyer makes use of such a device, the manufacturer is considered to be a contributory infringer.

Infringing a Design Patent

Infringement upon a design patent differs from infringement upon other types of patents. The scope of rights provided by a design patent is dependent upon the drawings that accompany the patent, not the claims of the patent. Infringement is assessed by whether the appearance of the infringing design is substantially the same as the design claimed by the drawings of the patented invention. Design patent infringement is measured by the Gorham test. The Gorham test determines whether an ordinary consumer finds the patented and the infringing design to be similar such that their resemblance is considered to be deceptive to the consumer and induces the consumer to make purchase of the object containing the infringing design. The two designs must not only be similar, the infringing design must contain the novel features of the patented design. Novel features include those design features of a patented article that distinguish it from prior art.

Design patents protect an article's ornamental and nonfunctional features. The patent may not be used to protect the functional features of the article for which the patent is obtained. A design patent, for example, may protect the unique design attached to an article of clothing. However, a design patent does not protect the manner in which the design is attached. The most common defense in a case of design patent infringement is that the patented design lacks the requirement to be an ornamental and thus, is an invalid patent. The argument is usually based on the contention that the design is of no concern to consumers.

Markman Hearing

Infringement, for other than design patents, is determined as it relates to the scope of coverage for the infringed upon claims. The language used to document a claim in a patent application defines the scope of the claim. As such, the language of a claim is open to interpretation of the reader. Both the patent owner and the infringing party are allowed to present their interpretation of claims to a judge in what is termed a Markman hearing. This hearing is held prior to taking the issue to trial. During the Markman hearing, the judge decides the scope of each presented claim. If the language of a claim is ambiguous, the description, drawings, and if necessary the entire patent application file may be used by the judge to interpret the claim. The judge may also receive expert testimony to assist in interpreting the claim.

Court Hearing

Infringement is a matter that must be brought before a federal court, except when the infringing invention is being imported into the United States. If the invention is being imported, the patent owner may also bring proceedings before the International Trade Commission to halt the transport of the invention at its port of entry into the United States. The location of a federal court hearing is established as the federal court located in the district of the defendant's residence or the district where the defendant committed the infringing act and has a regular and established place of business. The defendant is the infringing party. The patent owner must decide which federal district court is in the geographic location, known as venue, appropriate to handle the particular case of infringement. It is common for patent owners to bring suit against a retailer or customer to establish venue closest to his or her own residence. Manufacturers have the burden of defending customers and retailers in infringement lawsuits regardless of whether the manufacturer is local to the residence of the party they are defending. If the defendant is a corporation, the residence of the corporation is any district where the corporation is incorporated, doing business, or is licensed to do business. If the defendant is the federal government or a contractor under a federal contract, the lawsuit must be brought before the U.S. Court of Federal Claims in Washington, D.C. Patent owners are entitled to sue the government for infringement and receive compensation for loss of use incurred as a result of use by or for the government. In 1999, the Supreme Court ruled that under Constitutional principles, states could not be held liable for patent infringement.

The plaintiff in an infringement lawsuit must prepare three particular documents and file them with the appropriate federal court. The federal court's rules of service and process also dictate that a copy of each document must also be delivered to the defendant.

1. **A complaint.** The complaint sets forth the facts of the infringement and requests remedies, such as compensation or an injunction. If the plaintiff desires a jury trial, that request must also be included.

2. **A summons.**

3. **A civil cover sheet.**

The defendant must file a response to the complaint in which the defendant denies or admits the accusations and provides a listing of defenses to such. If the plaintiff did not request a jury trial, but the defendant would like to have such a trial, it must be requested with the answer to the complaint. If the defendant wishes to file a counterclaim against the plaintiff, the counterclaim must also be filed at the same time that the answer is filed. If an act, which is cause for a counterclaim, arises out of the same occurrence or transaction that is the subject of the complaint, it must be filed as the counterclaim. Such a counterclaim is compulsory. As an example, a patent owner commits battery against the company CEO that he believes is infringing on the patented invention. If the patent owner then files an infringement lawsuit against the company, the company CEO must file a claim for damages as a counterclaim in his or her answer to the patent owner's complaint.

An appropriate federal district court will examine the claims of the patented invention against the infringing device or process. A patent owner may request that the court issue an injunction to prevent any further infringement of the patent and request an award of monetary damages for the infringement. Should a party be found guilty of infringing upon the rights granted by a patent, the patent owner is awarded damages to compensate for the loss incurred by the infringement.

Damages for design and plant patents are generally awarded at reasonably assessed royalty rates that are based on the amount of loss in profits due to the infringement. The court, for example, may award damages as the amount of royalty payments the patent owner would have received had the patent owner licensed the sale of the infringing device. If the infringement is found to be deliberate and in bad faith, the amount of reasonably assessed royalties may be tripled. This is known as enhanced damages. The infringer may also be ordered to pay the patent holder's legal fees. When the infringing party is the federal government or a contractor to the federal government, compensation is limited to damages plus interest. Damages for utility patents may not include profits resulting from infringement.

The infringing party may be issued an injunction that specifically orders a halt to making, selling, or using the invention. A court order may halt the manufacture and sale of a patented invention even if the invention has not been properly marked with the patent number. The patent owner may request a preliminary injunction that halts the immediate activity before a trial begins, a permanent injunction that is granted at the end of a court trial, or a temporary restraining order that halts the activity for a short period of time. When a temporary restraining order or preliminary injunction is ordered, the plaintiff is required to post a bond, which is intended to cover costs and damages should the defendant prevail in the lawsuit. Temporary restraining orders may be issued without notice to the infringing party if it is concluded that immediate damages will result from the infringing activity. As an example, that court is convinced that evidence of an infringement would be destroyed. A temporary restraining order is issued and remains in effect until the court is able to schedule a hearing for a preliminary injunction. During the preliminary injunction hearing, both parties present their evidence to the court. A preliminary injunction is ordered if it is determined that the plaintiff is likely to prevail in the lawsuit and the plaintiff is likely to suffer irreparable damage if the injunction is not ordered. A preliminary injunction remains in effect until a final injunction or judgment is issued. The patent owner may not obtain a court order to halt the government infringement.

The district court decision may be appealed to the Court of Appeals for the Federal Circuit. Any decision handed by the Court of Appeals may then be appealed to the Supreme Court by writ of certiorari.

Stopping Infringement

While federal district courts have the final say in issues of infringement, alternative methods may be effective in stopping infringement. The resolution of a case of infringement does not have to result in a legal suit. According to the American Intellectual Property Law Association, the estimated median cost of patent litigation is $280,000 up to the trial and $518,000 through trial. Because of the expense of litigation, many patent owners prefer to resolve issues of patent infringement without going to trial. A patent owner may engage in any of the following methods in an effort to stop an infringement:

File an Infringement Action in the Appropriate Federal District Court

Filing an infringement action in federal court is the most effective and final method of stopping infringement, but it is also the more costly and time-consuming method. The federal court process involves five phases.

1. **Temporary Relief.** During the temporary relief phase of the process, a patent owner attempts to obtain a temporary court order that restrains the infringing party from performing some act, pending further litigation.

2. **Discovery.** During the discovery phase, both parties to the suit issue one another interrogatories, which are requests for admissions or documents and depositions of prospective witnesses. Interrogatories are formal or written questions to a witness, which require an answer declared under oath. Depositions are interviews to give testimony or evidence under oath. Discovery is an expensive phase of the process and is often responsible for causing parties to come to some sort of settlement. A discovery may also request information about the patented or infringing invention that is confidential. The parties are allowed to engage in an agreement to protect and limit the disclosure of such information. Furthermore, the court may issue a

protective order that prohibits public disclosure of such confidential information.

3. **Summary.** During the summary phase, both parties try to obtain a decision as to some key issue, or the patent owner tries to obtain an injunction against an infringing activity. Also during this phase the parties may be court-mandated to arbitration, or they may voluntarily submit to arbitration.

4. **Trial.** During the trial phase, the matter goes to trail before a jury or judge. However, a Supreme Court ruling dictates that a jury may not interpret patent claims of an invention. Only the judge may make such an interpretation. The jury may, however, make a determination as to whether infringement has occurred and the amount of damages to be awarded. Expert witnesses and visual aides are often introduced to assist the judge or jury in interpreting the technical terms and scientific language that may characterize an invention. Each party must identify its expert witnesses prior to the trial by filing an Identification of Expert Witness document with the court. Visual aides, such as enlarged copies of claims, may be used to simplify procedures. Charts may also be used to compare claims to the invention or to illustrate a sequence of steps. After a verdict is issued, the judge must confirm the verdict before a judgment can be enforced. In some instances, the judge may set aside a jury's verdict if the judge determines that laws and facts do not properly support the verdict.

5. **Appeal.** During the appeal phase, a dissatisfied party appeals the decision of the district court to a higher court, the U.S. Court of Appeals for the Federal Circuit (CAFC). The CAFC is in Washington D.C., but often travels around the country to hear appeals. The CAFC provides for a three-member panel of judges to review the trial records

and determine if a legal error has occurred. If either of the parties is not satisfied with the decision of the CAFC, an appeal may be filed with the U.S. Supreme Court. The Supreme Court rarely hears cases of patent infringement; as such, the CAFC ruling is usually the final ruling on infringement. In some instances, the decision of the CAFC may lead to a new trial.

Expending resources in the initial phases of the process may lead to a successful outcome of winning a temporary relief order against the infringing party or winning an injunction during the summary phase. These outcomes may be responsible to bring the issue of infringement to a close before it goes to trial.

Engage an Infringement Action under a Special Procedure

Special procedures have been established to handle infringement issues that are less costly and time consuming than the federal court process. Federal and state laws provide criminal penalties for some types of infringement. These laws are not specifically designed to protect patents, but patent owners who also have copyrights, trade secrets, and trademarks attached to their inventions may be able to make use of these laws to intervene an infringing action. Federal anti-privacy laws provide for punishment of copyright infringement when the infringement offers a commercial advantage or provides financial gain. Federal laws also impose punishment for the reproduction of recordings or trafficking of counterfeit recordings, software, and motion pictures. If an infringing party attempts to import copyrighted or trademarked merchandise, the copyright owner or trademark owner may register the copyright, company identifier, or mark with the U.S. Customs Service and have the merchandise seized. If such a seizure takes place, the owner of the seized merchandise will have to appear in court where it will be determined whether the goods should be released to the original addressee or destroyed. States have statutes that guard against the misappropriation of trade secrets and industrial espionage. If the infringer attempts to import counterfeit merchandise into the United States, the patent owner may request an order of the International Trade Commission, which will ban the importation. The ITC will examine the validity of the patent and decide whether the infringing importation has an anti-competitive impact on U.S. commerce. ITC proceedings are less expensive and much quicker than those used in a court of law.

Issue a Cease and Desist Notice to the Infringing Party

A patent owner may have an attorney send the infringing party a cease and desist letter, which demands an immediate halt to infringing acts, demands an accounting of all illegal sales and requests payment to reimburse losses due to the past infringement. The letter may also offer a threat of litigation if the infringing activity is not halted. In response, the infringing party may do any of the following:

- Ignore the letter.
- Make contact to seek an amicable solution.
- Defend his or her actions in court.

Ignoring the letter is the most frequent action to be taken in such situations. The patent owner would then have to resort to another method of stopping the infringement. If the infringer makes contact to seek a solution, the solution is likely to entail reneging on the payment of damages in return for a halt of infringing activities. If the infringer decides to defend his or her actions in court, the infringer will institute a declaratory relief action. The issuance of a cease and desist letter provides the infringer with reasonable cause to believe that he or she will be sued. An infringer may initiate a declaratory relief lawsuit if the infringer has reasonable belief that an infringement lawsuit will be filed.

Declaratory relief is a request to determine the validity of a patent and determine whether the patent has actually been infringed. The infringer becomes the plaintiff in the lawsuit and insists that he or she has not committed an infringing act or insists that the issued IP right is invalid. This method of stopping infringement may become costly since the infringer is likely to file action in his or her district and the patent owner will have to bear the expense of defending the suit in that particular district.

Negotiate a Settlement with the Infringing Party

Negotiating a compromise with the infringing party is the most sensible alternative to resolving infringement issues in most situations. An offer to negotiate a settlement is not considered a threat of litigation and the infringing party may not initiate a lawsuit for declaratory judgment as a result of receipt of such an offer. A settlement offer may also provide the patent owner with less money than would be demanded in a court judgment. The settlement may include any of the following:

- Reneging on the payment of damages in exchange for a halt of the infringing activity.

- Grant of a narrow non-exclusive license to the infringer party so long as the infringement does not involve a commercial identifier.

- A reverse license, which gives the infringing party permission to continue manufacture and sales so long as royalty payments are made for all past and future sales.

In most cases of infringement or alleged infringement, neither the patent owner nor the accused party wants to engage in expensive litigation. A negotiated settlement offers many advantages that save both parties the expense of litigation and the time necessary to complete the litigation process. Litigation may continue for two or three years when the courts are involved. Furthermore, the payout for a settlement is a guaranteed payment, which does not require enforcement and collection.

A settlement requires that a contract be signed and executed between the parties involved. Some states have very specific requirements regarding settlement agreements and contracts. Very specific language must be included in the contract to protect the rights of all parties. In some instances, the terms of a settlement agreement must be presented in what is termed a stipulated judgment. A stipulated judgment is a document that must be filed with the courts.

A settlement offer may be reached in privacy through informal procedures known as mediation or arbitration. Meditation requires the disputing parties submit their arguments to an impartial mediator who assists in reaching a settlement. Arbitration is sought if mediation fails. Arbitration involves referring the dispute to one or more impartial individuals. Arbitration may be initiated by an agreement or by submission from the parties of the dispute. The American Arbitration Association establishes Patent Arbitration Rules and has established a panel of arbitrators. The decision reached during arbitration is usually the final and binding decision. The International Chamber of Commerce in Stockholm or the London Court of Arbitration governs international arbitration.

Companies exist that provide patent enforcement litigation services to patent owners. In return for an agreed upon annual premium, these companies will reimburse part or all of the cost of litigation, dependent upon the limits established by the insurance policy. One company, Patent Enforcement Fund, will provide patent enforcement litigation services in return for a partial interest in the patent. Such insurance coverage may be initiated during the patent application pendency period. Likewise, businesses may be insured against patent infringement through their business liability insurance.

Defending Patent Infringement

When a party is sued for infringing a patented invention, that party should assert a defense if he or she believes it is applicable. A defense asserted without merit or based on falsehoods may destroy the defendant's credibility and lead to sanctions or even imprisonment if felony perjury is charged. The defendant in a patent lawsuit is most likely to argue that either an established patent is invalid or that his or her invention does not infringe. Other arguments may include the infringement should be excused, the patent owner misused the patent or the patent owner has unclean hands. Some typical defenses to support such arguments include the following:

- **Invalidity.** The invalidity of a patent is usually based on a lack of novelty or non-obviousness. The PTO may be requested to reexamine any patent that is already in force. The criterion used by the PTO in granting the patent is reexamined in an attempt to show that the PTO was incorrect in granting the patent. The defendant will attempt to show that prior art exists that renders the patent obvious or the defendant will attempt to show that the invention was offered for sale, sold, or otherwise disclosed more than one year before the patent application was filed. After reexamination, the PTO issues either a certificate of patentability or a certificate of unpatentability.

- **Inequitable Conduct.** In establishing inequitable conduct, the defendant attempts to establish that a patent owner intentionally misled the PTO or withheld material information that would have affected the patent examination process.

- **Patent misuse.** A defendant may argue that a patent owner misused the rights afforded by a patent and therefore cannot sue for infringement. Common types of misuse include involvement in unethical business practices or violations of antitrust laws. A tie-in is also considered a patent misuse. A tie-is the illegal act of obligating a licensee to purchase another product that is beyond the scope of the licensor's IP rights. A patent owner who engages in a tie-in may not sue for infringement. The Patent Misuse Amendments Act of 1988 requires that courts apply a "rule of reason" and view all relevant factors to determine if a tie-in arrangement is in any way justified.

- **Lack of standing.** It may be argued that the patent owner lacks the legal capacity, also termed standing, to bring the lawsuit. In such a case, the defendant would need to prove that he or she, not the plaintiff, is the true owner of the patented invention.

- **File Wrapper Estoppel.** The official file of a patent that is held at the PTO is known as a file wrapper. A file wrapper contains all correspondence, statements, admissions, and documents related to a patented invention. When a patent applicant makes certain admissions or disclaims certain rights relative to the invention, they become part of the file wrapper. Another party may create a similar invention by exploiting such rights and admissions and then design around the patented invention. The patent owner may not sue for infringement over rights disclaimed in the file wrapper. So long as the invention does not infringe under the doctrine of equivalents, the invention does not constitute an infringement. This defense is known as file wrapper estoppel. Estoppel means prevented from contradicting a former statement or action.

This is similar to a defense known as a reverse doctrine of equivalents or negative doctrine of equivalents. Under this defense, a device that would otherwise constitute literal infringement is excused because the infringing device has a different function or produces a different result from the patented invention.

- **Exhaustion Doctrine.** Rights to a patented invention are exhausted after the item is sold. The item may then be resold at the will of the purchaser and no infringement occurs. This defense is also known as the "First Sale Doctrine." The doctrine does not apply in situations where an infringing invention is sold without authorization from the patent owner and then resold.

- **Experimental use.** Patent laws allow for the use of a patented invention if the use encourages competition and speeds the release of human health care and certain animal products. The otherwise infringement is allowed when the use of the patented invention is necessary to obtain regulatory approval. The experimental use defense is employed when a patented invention is necessary for research or development of drugs to cure a disease.

- **Repair doctrine.** The repair doctrine dictates that it is not infringement to repair a patented invention or replace components of a patented invention. The doctrine further dictates that it is not infringement, contributory or otherwise, to sell materials to be used for such repair or replacement. The doctrine does not apply to the complete rebuilding of an unauthorized invention or items made or sold without authorization from the patent owner. A specially designed ergonomic chair, for example, may be patented, but the fabric used for the chair is not patented. The repair doctrine provides for the sale of fabric to purchasers of the patented chair. If another company made and sold an infringing version of the chair, any fabric sold to replace or repair the infringing chair would be considered contributory infringement.

- **Claim methods.** In 1999, patent laws were amended to provide a defense that is only applicable to patents that claim methods of accomplishing a process, also termed method claim patents. If a process is invented and a defendant engages in the commercial use of a product produced by the method at least one year before the filing of a method claim patent, the patent may be considered invalid as a defense against infringement.

- **Laches.** Laches is waiting an unreasonable amount of time to file a lawsuit. There exists no statute of limitation for filing an infringement lawsuit. However, monetary damages can only be recovered for infringement that occurred in the six years prior to filing a lawsuit. Despite the lack of statute, most courts will not permit a patent owner to sue for infringement if the patent owner laches. Most courts adopt the six-year time as a reasonable time within which to file suit. Generally, if a patent owner laches for more than six years, courts will dismiss the lawsuit unless the patent owner is able to provide a reasonable basis for the delay.

Conclusion

The process of patenting an invention can be a very time consuming, complex, and expensive method of protecting the invention. The complications of designing and developing the invention are only the start of the process, though it is obviously one of the most important parts of the process. It is important to complement design and development efforts with adequate documentation of the invention to increase the level of protection for the invention. An invention needs to be documented from the time of its conception to the development of a prototype, working model, or working process.

The process of filing application for patent protection offers its own complexities and for most new and first-time inventors, the services of competent patent professionals may be needed to ensure that any subsequently issued patent provides coverage sufficient to protect the invention against infringement, design around and theft.

The PTO has established requirements for patents that must be met as well as dates and timelines which, if not adhered to, may disallow the issuance of a patent or cause any issued patent to be voided. In most instances, additional forms and documentation are required to prepare a complete patent application package. To provide the broadest form of patent protection, claims of an invention's functionality must be documented in the patent application, and they must be presented in legal form so as to withstand opposition in litigation, if it becomes necessary.

A working, patented invention will not generate profits for an inventor. The goal of generating profits cannot be reached until the inventor is capable of manufacturing, distributing, and selling the invention. This part of the patenting process offers more complexities. Finding an appropriate manufacturer and distributor or successfully self-manufacturing and distributing an invention can mean the difference between generating profits or suffering loss for an invention.

Bibliography

1. *From Patent To Profit: Secrets & Strategies For The Successful Inventor, Third Edition*

2. *How To Make Patent Drawings Yourself: A Patent It Yourself Companion*

3. *Patent It Yourself*

4. *Patents and How to Get One: A Practical Handbook*

5. *Patents, Copyrights & Trademarks for Dummies*

6. Pressman David & Stim Richard. *Nolo's Patents for Beginners.* Berkley, CA: Nolo, 2004

7. *The Entrepreneur's Guide to Patents, Copyrights, Trademarks, Trade Secrets & Licensing*

8. *The Inventor's Notebook: A Patent It Yourself Companion*

Appendices

APPENDIX I: US PTO FEE SCHEDULE

Fee Code	37 CFR	Description	Fee	Small Entity Fee (if applicable)
UNITED STATES PATENT AND TRADEMARK OFFICE FY 2006 FEE SCHEDULE Effective December 8, 2004* (revisions effective May 15, 2006)				
Patent Application Filing Fees				
1011/2011	1.16(a)(1)	Basic filing fee - Utility *filed on or after December 8, 2004*	300.00	150.00
4011‡	1.16(a)(1)	Basic filing fee - Utility (electronic filing for small entities) *filed on or after December 8, 2004*	n/a	75.00
1001/2001	1.16(a)(2)	Basic filing fee – Utility *filed before December 8, 2004*	790.00	395.00
1201/2201	1.16(h)	Independent claims in excess of three	200.00	100.00
1202/2202	1.16(i)	Claims in excess of 20	50.00	25.00
1203/2203	1.16(j)	Multiple dependent claim	360.00	180.00
1051/2051	1.16(f)	Surcharge - Late filing fee, search fee, examination fee or oath or declaration	130.00	65.00
1081/2081	1.16(s)	Utility Application Size Fee - for each additional 50 sheets that exceeds 100 sheets	250.00	125.00
1012/2012	1.16(b)(1)	Basic filing fee – Design *filed on or after December 8, 2004*	200.00	100.00
1002/2002	1.16(b)(2)	Basic filing fee - Design *filed before December 8, 2004*	350.00	175.00
1017/2017	1.16(b)(1)	Basic filing fee - Design (CPA) *filed on or after December 8, 2004*	200.00	100.00
1007/2007	1.16(b)(2)	Basic filing fee - Design (CPA) *filed before December 8, 2004*	350.00	175.00
1082/2082	1.16(s)	Design Application Size Fee - for each additional 50 sheets that exceeds 100 sheets	250.00	125.00
1013/2013	1.16(c)(1)	Basic filing fee - Plant *filed on or after December 8, 2004*	200.00	100.00
1003/2003	1.16(c)(2)	Basic filing fee - Plant *filed before December 8, 2004*	550.00	275.00
1083/2083	1.16(s)	Plant Application Size Fee - for each additional 50 sheets that exceeds 100 sheets	250.00	125.00
1014/2014	1.16(e)(1)	Basic filing fee - Reissue *filed on or after December 8, 2004*	300.00	150.00
1004/2004	1.16(e)(2)	Basic filing fee - Reissue *filed before December 8, 2004*	790.00	395.00
1019/2019	1.16(e)(1)	Basic filing fee - Design Reissue (CPA) *filed on or after December 8, 2004*	300.00	150.00
1009/2009	1.16(e)(2)	Basic filing fee - Design Reissue (CPA) *filed before December 8, 2004*	790.00	395.00

1204/2204	1.16(h)	Reissue independent claims in excess of three	200.00	100.00
1205/2205	1.16(i)	Reissue claims in excess of 20	50.00	25.00
1084/2084	1.16(s)	Reissue Application Size Fee - for each additional 50 sheets that exceeds 100 sheets	250.00	125.00
1005/2005	1.16(d)	Provisional application filing fee	200.00	100.00
1085/2085	1.16(s)	Provisional Application Size Fee - for each additional 50 sheets that exceeds 100 sheets	250.00	125.00
1052/2052	1.16(g)	Surcharge - Late provisional filing fee or cover sheet	50.00	25.00
1053	1.17(i)	Non-English specification	130.00	
† The 4000 series fee code may be used via EFS at http://www.uspto.gov/ebc/efs/index.html				
Patent Search Fees				
1111/2111	1.16(k)	Utility Search Fee	500.00	250.00
1112/2112	1.16(l)	Design Search Fee	100.00	50.00
1113/2113	1.16(m)	Plant Search Fee	300.00	150.00
1114/2114	1.16(n)	Reissue Search Fee	500.00	250.00
Patent Examination Fees				
1311/2311	1.16(o)	Utility Examination Fee	200.00	100.00
1312/2312	1.16(p)	Design Examination Fee	130.00	65.00
1313/2313	1.16(q)	Plant Examination Fee	160.00	80.00
1314/2314	1.16(r)	Reissue Examination Fee	600.00	300.00
Patent Post-Allowance Fees				
1501/2501	1.18(a)	Utility issue fee	1,400.00	700.00
1502/2502	1.18(b)	Design issue fee	800.00	400.00
1503/2503	1.18(c)	Plant issue fee	1,100.00	550.00
1511/2511	1.18(a)	Reissue issue fee	1,400.00	700.00
1504	1.18(d)	Publication fee for early, voluntary, or normal publication	300.00	
1505	1.18(d)	Publication fee for republication	300.00	
Patent Maintenance Fees				
1551/2551	1.20(e)	Due at 3.5 years	900.00	450.00
1552/2552	1.20(f)	Due at 7.5 years	2,300.00	1,150.00
1553/2553	1.20(g)	Due at 11.5 years	3,800.00	1,900.00
1554/2554	1.20(h)	Surcharge - 3.5 year - Late payment within 6 months	130.00	65.00
1555/2555	1.20(h)	Surcharge - 7.5 year - Late payment within 6 months	130.00	65.00
1556/2556	1.20(h)	Surcharge - 11.5 year - Late payment within 6 months	130.00	65.00
1557	1.20(i)(1)	Surcharge after expiration - Late payment is unavoidable	700.00	
1558	1.20(i)(2)	Surcharge after expiration - Late payment is unintentional	1,640.00	
Miscellaneous Patent Fees				
1801/2801	1.17(e)	Request for continued examination (RCE) (see 37 CFR 1.114)	790.00	395.00
1808	1.17(i)	Processing fee, except in provisional applications	130.00	

1803	1.17(i)	Request for voluntary publication or republication	130.00	
1802	1.17(k)	Request for expedited examination of a design application	900.00	
1804	1.17(n)	Request for publication of SIR - Prior to examiner's action	920.00*	
1805	1.17(o)	Request for publication of SIR - After examiner's action	1,840.00*	
1806	1.17(p)	Submission of an Information Disclosure Statement	180.00	
1807	1.17(q)	Processing fee for provisional applications	50.00	
1809/2809	1.17(r)	Filing a submission after final rejection (see 37 CFR 1.129(a))	790.00	395.00
1810/2810	1.17(s)	For each additional invention to be examined (see 37 CFR 1.129(b))	790.00	395.00
*Reduced by basic filing fee paid.				
Post Issuance Fees				
1811	1.20(a)	Certificate of correction	100.00	
1812	1.20(c)(1)	Request for ex parte reexamination	2,520.00	
1813	1.20(c)(2)	Request for inter partes reexamination	8,800.00	
1821/2821	1.20(c)(3)	Reexamination independent claims in excess of three and also in excess of the number of such claims in the patent under reexamination	200.00	100.00
1822/2822	1.20(c)(4)	Reexamination claims in excess of twenty and also in excess of the number of claims in the patent under reexamination	50.00	25.00
1814/2814	1.20(d)	Statutory disclaimer	130.00	65.00
Patent Extension of Time Fees				
1251/2251	1.17(a)(1)	Extension for response within first month	120.00	60.00
1252/2252	1.17(a)(2)	Extension for response within second month	450.00	225.00
1253/2253	1.17(a)(3)	Extension for response within third month	1,020.00	510.00
1254/2254	1.17(a)(4)	Extension for response within fourth month	1,590.00	795.00
1255/2255	1.17(a)(5)	Extension for response within fifth month	2,160.00	1,080.00
Patent Appeals/Interference Fees				
1401/2401	41.20(b)(1)	Notice of appeal	500.00	250.00
1402/2402	41.20(b)(2)	Filing a brief in support of an appeal	500.00	250.00
1403/2403	41.20(b)(3)	Request for oral hearing	1,000.00	500.00
Patent Petition Fees				
1462	1.17(f)	Petitions requiring the petition fee set forth in 37 CFR 1.17(f) (Group I)	400.00	
1463	1.17(g)	Petitions requiring the petition fee set forth in 37 CFR 1.17(g) (Group II)	200.00	
1464	1.17(h)	Petitions requiring the petition fee set forth in 37 CFR 1.17(h) (Group III)	130.00	
1451	1.17(j)	Petition to institute a public use proceeding	1,510.00	
1452/2452	1.17(l)	Petition to revive unavoidably abandoned application	500.00	250.00
1453/2453	1.17(m)	Petition to revive unintentionally abandoned application	1,500.00	750.00

1454	1.17(t)	Acceptance of an unintentionally delayed claim for priority	1,370.00	
1455	1.18(e)	Filing an application for patent term adjustment	200.00	
1456	1.18(f)	Request for reinstatement of term reduced	400.00	
1457	1.20(j)(1)	Extension of term of patent	1,120.00	
1458	1.20(j)(2)	Initial application for interim extension (see 37 CFR 1.790)	420.00	
1459	1.20(j)(3)	Subsequent application for interim extension (see 37 CFR 1.790)	220.00	
PCT Fees - National Stage				
1631/2631	1.492(a)	Basic National Stage Fee	300.00	150.00
1640/2640	1.492(b)(1)	National Stage Search Fee - U.S. was ISA or IPEA and all claims satisfy PCT Article 33(1)-(4)	0.00	0.00
1641/2641	1.492(b)(2)	National Stage Search Fee - U.S. was the ISA	100.00	50.00
1642/2642	1.492(b)(3)	National Stage Search Fee - search report prepared and provided to USPTO	400.00	200.00
1632/2632	1.492(b)(4)	National Stage Search Fee - all other situations	500.00	250.00
1643/2643	1.492(c)(1)	National Stage Examination Fee - U.S. was ISA or IPEA and, all claims satisfy PCT Article 33(1)-(4)	0.00	0.00
1633/2633	1.492(c)(2)	National Stage Examination Fee - all other situations	200.00	100.00
1614/2614	1.492(d)	Claims - extra independent (over three)	200.00	100.00
1615/2615	1.492(e)	Claims - extra total (over twenty)	50.00	25.00
1616/2616	1.492(f)	Claims - multiple dependent	360.00	180.00
1681/2681	1.492(j)	National Stage Application Size Fee - for each additional 50 sheets that exceeds 100 sheets	250.00	125.00
1617/2617	1.492(h)	Search fee, examination fee or oath or declaration after thirty months from priority date	130.00	65.00
1618	1.492(i)	English translation after thirty months from priority date	130.00	
PCT Fees - International Stage				
1601	1.445(a)(1)	Transmittal fee	300.00	
1602	1.445(a)(2)	PCT search fee - no prior U.S. application filed under 35 USC 111(a)	1,000.00	
1603	1.445(a)(2)	PCT search - prior U.S. application filed under 35 USC 111(a) with basic filing fee under 37CFR 1.16(a) paid; identified at time of filing international application	300.00	
1604	1.445(a)(3)	Supplemental search fee per additional invention	1,000.00	
1605	1.482(a)(1)	Preliminary examination fee - U.S. was the ISA	600.00	
1606	1.482(a)(1)	Preliminary examination fee -U.S. was not the ISA	750.00	

1607	1.482(a)(2)	Supplemental examination fee per additional invention	600.00	
1619		Late payment fee	variable	
1621		Transmitting application to Intl. Bureau to act as receiving office	300.00	
** Fee only applies to international applications filed prior to January 1, 2004. PCT Fees to Foreign Offices***				
1701		International filing fee (first 30 pages) - PCT Easy	1,008.00	
1702		International filing fee (first 30 pages)	1,086.00	
1703		Supplemental international filing fee (for each page over 30)	12.00	
1704		International search (EPO)	1,925.00	
1709		International search (KIPO)	232.00	
1705		Handling fee	155.00	
1706		Handling Fee – 75 percent reduction. if applicant, or two or more applicants each meet criteria specified at: <http://www.wipo.int/pct/en/fees/fee_reduction.pdf>	38.75	
1708		International CD applications	4,800.00	
*** PCT Fees to Foreign Offices subject to periodic change due to fluctuations in exchange rate. Refer to the Official Gazette of the United States Patent and Trademark Office for current amounts.				
Patent Service Fees				
8001	1.19(a)(1)	Printed copy of patent w/o color, delivery by USPS, USPTO Box, or electronic means	3.00	
8003	1.19(a)(2)	Printed copy of plant patent in color	15.00	
8004	1.19(a)(3)	Color copy of patent (other than plant patent) or SIR containing a color drawing	25.00	
8005	1.19(a)(1)	Patent Application Publication (PAP)	3.00	
8007	1.19(b)(1)(i)(A)	Copy of patent application as filed	20.00	
8008	1.19(b)(1)(i)(B)	Copy of patent-related file wrapper and contents of 400 or fewer pages, if provided on paper	200.00	
8009	1.19(b)(1)(i)(C)	Additional fee for each additional 100 pages of patent-related file wrapper and (paper) contents, or portion thereof	40.00	
8010	1.19(b)(1)(i)(D)	Individual application documents, other than application as filed, per document	25.00	
8011	1.19(b)(1)(ii)(B)	Copy of patent-related file wrapper and contents if provided electronically or on a physical electronic medium as specified in 1.19(b)(1)(ii)	55.00	
8012	1.19(b)(1)(ii)(C)	Additional fee for each continuing physical electronic medium in single order of 1.19(b)(1)(ii)(B)	15.00	

8041	1.19(b)(2)(i)(A)	Copy of patent-related file wrapper contents that were submitted and are stored on compact disk or other electronic form (e.g., compact disks stored in Artifact folder), other than as available in 1.19(b)(1); first physical electronic medium in a single order	55.00	
8042	1.19(b)(2)(i)(B)	Additional fee for each continuing copy of patent-related file wrapper contents as specified in 1.19(b)(2)(i)(A)	15.00	
8043	1.19(b)(2)(ii)	Copy of patent-related file wrapper contents that were submitted and are stored on compact disk, or other electronic form, other than as available in 1.19(b)(1); if provided electronically other than on a physical electronic medium, per order	55.00	
8013	1.19(b)(3)	Copy of office records, except copies of applications as filed	25.00	
8014	1.19(b)(4)	For assignment records, abstract of title and certification, per patent	25.00	
8904	1.19(c)	Library service	50.00	
8015	1.19(d)	List of U.S. patents and SIRs in subclass	3.00	
8016	1.19(e)	Uncertified statement re status of maintenance fee payments	10.00	
8017	1.19(f)	Copy of non-U.S. document	25.00	
8050	1.19(g)	Petitions for documents in form other than that provided by this part, or in form other than that generally provided by Director, to be decided in accordance with merits	AT COST	
8018	1.21(c)	Disclosure document filing fee	10.00	
8019	1.21(d)	Local delivery box rental, annually	50.00	
8020	1.21(e)	International type search report	40.00	
8902	1.21(g)	Self-service copy charge, per page	0.25	
8021	1.21(h)	Recording each patent assignment, agreement or other paper, per property	40.00	
8022	1.21(i)	Publication in Official Gazette	25.00	
8023	1.21(j)	Labor charges for services, per hour or fraction thereof	40.00	
8024	1.21(k)	Unspecified other services, excluding labor	AT COST	
8025	1.21(l)	Retaining abandoned application	130.00	
8026	1.21(n)	Handling fee for incomplete or improper application	130.00	
8027	1.296	Handling fee for withdrawal of SIR	130.00	
Patent Enrollment Fees				
9001	1.21(a)(1)(i)	Application fee (non-refundable)	40.00	
9003	1.21(a)(2)	Registration to practice or grant of limited recognition under §11.9(b) or (c)	100.00	
9004	1.21(a)(3)	Reinstatement to practice	40.00	
9005	1.21(a)(4)	Certificate of good standing as an attorney or agent	10.00	
9006	1.21(a)(4)	Certificate of good standing as an attorney or agent, suitable for framing	20.00	

9010	1.21(a)(1)(ii)(A)	For test administration by commercial entity	200.00	
9011	1.21(a)(1)(ii)(B)	For test administration by the USPTO	450.00	
9012	1.21(a)(5)(i)	Review of decision by the Director of Enrollment and Discipline under §11.2(c)	130.00	
9013	1.21(a)(5)(ii)	Review of decision of the Director of Enrollment and Discipline under §11.2(d)	130.00	
9014	1.21(a)(10)	Application fee for person disciplined, convicted of a felony or certain misdemeanors under §11.7(h)	1,600.00	Back to top>
GENERAL FEES				
Finance Service Fees				
9201	1.21(b)(1) or 2.6(b)(13)(i)	Establish deposit account	10.00	
9202	1.21(b)(2) or 2.6(b)(13)(ii)	Service charge for below minimum balance	25.00	
9202	1.21(b)(3)	Service charge for below minimum balance restricted subscription deposit account	25.00	
9101	1.21(m) or 2.6(b)(12)	Processing each payment refused or charged back	50.00	
Computer Service Fees				
8031/8531		Computer records	AT COST	
Trademark Processing Fees ****				
6001	2.6(a)(1)(i)	Application for registration, per international class (paper filing)	375.00	
7001	2.6(a)(1)(ii)	Application for registration, per international class (electronic filing, TEAS application)	325.00	
7007	2.6(a)(1)(iii)	Application for registration, per international class (electronic filing, TEAS Plus application)	275.00	
6002/7002	2.6(a)(2)	Filing an Amendment to Allege Use under §1(c), per class	100.00	
6003/7003	2.6(a)(3)	Filing a Statement of Use under §1(d)(1), per class	100.00	
6004/7004	2.6(a)(4)	Filing a Request for a Six-month Extension of Time for Filing a Statement of Use under §1(d)(1), per class	150.00	
6005/7005	2.6(a)(15)	Petitions to the Director	100.00	
6006	2.6(a)(19)	Dividing an application, per new application (file wrapper) created	100.00	
6008/7008	2.6(a)(1)(iv)	Additional fee for application that doesn't meet TEAS Plus filing requirements, per class	50.00	
6201/7201	2.6(a)(5)	Application for renewal, per class	400.00	
6203/7203	2.6(a)(6)	Additional fee for filing renewal application during grace period, per class	100.00	
6204	2.6(a)(21)	Correcting a deficiency in a renewal application	100.00	
6205/7205	2.6(a)(12)	Filing §8 affidavit, per class	100.00	

6206/7206	2.6(a)(14)	Additional fee for filing §8 affidavit during grace period, per class	100.00	
6207	2.6(a)(20)	Correcting a deficiency in a §8 affidavit	100.00	
6208/7208	2.6(a)(13)	Filing §15 affidavit, per class	200.00	
6210	2.6(a)(7)	Publication of mark under §12(c), per class	100.00	
6211	2.6(a)(8)	Issuing new certificate of registration	100.00	
6212	2.6(a)(9)	Certificate of correction, registrant's error	100.00	
6213	2.6(a)(10)	Filing disclaimer to registration	100.00	
6214	2.6(a)(11)	Filing amendment to registration	100.00	
6401/7401	2.6(a)(16)	Petition for cancellation, per class	300.00	
6402/7402	2.6(a)(17)	Notice of opposition, per class	300.00	
6403/7403	2.6(a)(18)	Ex parte appeal, per class	100.00	
Trademark Madrid Protocol Fees ****				
6901/7901	7.6(a)(1)	Certifying an International application based on single application or registration, per class	100.00	
6902/7902	7.6(a)(2)	Certifying an International application based on more than one basic application or registration, per class	150.00	
6903/7903	7.6(a)(3)	Transmitting a Request to Record an Assignment or restriction under 7.23 or 7.24	100.00	
6904/7904	7.6(a)(4)	Filing a Notice of Replacement, per class	100.00	
6905/7905	7.6(a)(5)	Filing an affidavit under 71 of the Act, per class	100.00	
6906/7906	7.6(a)(6)	Surcharge for filing affidavit under 71 of the Act during grace period, per class	100.00	
6907/7907	7.6(a)(7)	Transmitting a subsequent designation	100.00	
Trademark International Application Fees***				
7951	7.7(1)	International application fee	Reference CFR 7.7 for payment of fees to International Bureau (IB) and IB calculator at: <http://www.wipo.int/madrid/en>.	
7952	7.14(c)	Correcting irregularities in an International application		
7953	7.21	Subsequent designation fee		
7954	7.23	Recording of an assignment of an international registration under 7.23		

**** The 7000 series fee code (e.g., 7001, 7002, etc.) is used for electronic filing via TEAS, which is available at <www.uspto.gov/teas/>. In addition, the 6000 series fee codes under the Trademark Madrid Protocol Fees are being offered for use as a paper-based filing alternative.

Trademark Service Fees				
8501	2.6(b)(1)	Printed copy of registered mark, delivery by USPS, USPTO Box, or electronic means	3.00	
8503	2.6(b)(4)(i)	Certified copy of registered mark, with title and/or status, regular service	15.00	
8504	2.6(b)(4)(ii)	Certified copy of registered mark, with title and/or status, expedited local service	30.00	
8507	2.6(b)(2)	Certified copy of trademark application as filed	15.00	

8508	2.6(b)(3)	Certified or uncertified copy of trademark-related file wrapper and contents	50.00	
8513	2.6(b)(5)	Certified or uncertified copy of trademark document, unless otherwise provided	25.00	
8514	2.6(b)(7)	For assignment records, abstracts of title and certification per registration	25.00	
8902	2.6(b)(9)	Self-service copy charge, per page	0.25	
8521	2.6(b)(6)	Recording trademark assignment, agreement or other paper, first mark per document	40.00	
8522	2.6(b)(6)	For second and subsequent marks in the same document	25.00	
8523	2.6(b)(10)	Labor charges for services, per hour or fraction thereof	40.00	
8524	2.6(b)(11)	Unspecified other services, excluding labor	AT COST	
Fastener Quality Act Fees				
6991	2.7(a)	Recordal application fee	20.00	
6992	2.7(b)	Renewal application fee	20.00	
6993	2.7(c)	Late fee for renewal application	20.00	

* The effective date for the fee amounts in 37 CFR 2.6(a)(1)(i) and (a)(1)(ii) is January 31, 2005, and the effective date for the fee amounts in (a)(1)(iii) and (a)(1)(iv) is July 18, 2005.

The effective date for the fee amounts in 37 CFR 1.492(b)(1) and (c)(1) is July 1, 2005, and the effective date for the fee amounts in 37 CFR 1.492(b)(2) and (b)(3) is February 1, 2005.

The effective date for PCT Fees to Foreign Offices is March 1, 2005, except for fee code 1704, which is effective March 15, 2005.

APPENDIX II: U.S. COPYRIGHT OFFICE FEE SCHEDULE

Current fees charged by the U.S. Copyright Office are scheduled to change to the proposed amount, effective July 1, 2006.

Registration, Recordation, and Rated Services		
	Current	Proposed
Registration of a basic claim in an original work of authorship: Forms SE, TX, PA, VA (including Short Forms), and Form SR	$30	$45
Registration of a claim in a group of contribution to periodicals (GR/CP)	30	45
Registration of a renewal claim (Form RE): Claim without Addendum Addendum	60 30	75 220
Registration of a claim in a group of serials (Form SE/Group) [per issue, with minimum two issues]	15	25
Registration of a claim in a group of daily newspapers and qualified newsletters (Form G/DN)	55	70
Registration of a claim in a restored copyright (Form GATT)	30	45
Registration of a group of published photographs	30	45
Registration of a correction or amplification to a claim (Form CA)	100	115
Preregistration of certain unpublished works	100	100
Providing an additional certificate of registration	30	40
Certification of other Copyright Office records (per hour)	80	150
Search-report prepared from official records (per hour) Estimate of search fee	75 NA	150 100
Location of Copyright Office records (per hour) Location of in-process materials (per hour)	80 100	150 150
Recordation of document, including a Notice of Intention to Enforce (NIE) (single title) Additional titles (per group of 10 titles)	80 20	95 25
Recordation of Notice of Intention to Make and Distribute Phonorecords	12	12
Recordation of an Interim Designation of Agent to Receive Notification of Claimed Infringement under §512(c)(2) (Online Service Provider Designation)	30	80

Issuance of a receipt for a §407 deposit	10	20
Registration of a claim in a mask work (Form MW)	75	95
Registration of a claim in a vessel hull (Form DVH)	140	200

Special Services

	Current	Proposed
Special handling fee for a claim	$580	$685
Each additional claim using the same deposit	50	50
Special handling fee for recordation of a document	330	435
Expedited Reference and Bibliography search and report (per hour)	NA	400
Expedited Certification & Documents services (surcharge, per hour)	200	240
Requests for reconsideration:		
First request	200	250
Additional claim in related group	20	25
Second request	500	500
Additional claim in related group	20	25
Secure test processing charge, per hour	60	150
Copying of Copyright Office Records by staff:		
Photocopy (b&w) (per page, minimum $6)	.50	0.50
Photocopy (color) (per page, minimum $6)	1	1.50
Photograph (Polaroid)	10	
Photograph (digital)	30	45
Slide	2	3
Audiocassette (first 30 minutes)	50	75
Additional 15-minute increments	20	
Videocassette (first 30 minutes)	50	75
Additional 15 minute increments	25	25
CD or DVD	40	50
Zip or floppy disk	75	100

Handling fee of extra deposit copy for certification	30	45
Full-term retention of a published deposit	425	425
Notice to Libraries and Archives 　Each additional title	50 50	20 20
Use of COINS terminal in LM-B14 (per hour)	20	25
FedEx Service	15	35
Delivery of documents via facsimile (per page, seven-page maximum)	1	1
Service charge for deposit account overdraft	100	150
Service charge for dishonored deposit account replenishment check	35	75

Licensing Division Services		
	Current	**Proposed**
Recordation of a Notice of Intention to Make and Distribute Phonorecords (17 *USC* 115) (per title)	$12	$12
Filing Fee for Recordation of License Agreements under 17 *USC* 118	50	125
Recordation of Certain Contracts by Cable Television Systems Located Outside the 48 Contiguous States	50	50
Initial Notice of Digital Transmission of Sound Recording (17 *USC* 114) 　Amendment of 17 *USC* 114 Notice	20 20	20 20
Statement of Account Amendment (Cable Television Systems and Satellite Carriers, 17 *USC* 111 and 119)	15	95
Statement of Account Amendment (Digital Audio Recording Devices or Media, 17 *USC* 1003)	20	95
Photocopy made by staff (b&w) (per page, minimum $6)	0.40	0.50
Search, per hour	65	150
Certification of Search Report	65	150

APPENDIX III: MEMBER NATIONS OF THE PARIS CONVENTION

Paris Convention for the Protection of Industrial Property

Paris Convention (1883), revised at Brussels (1900), Washington (1911), The Hague (1925), London (1934), Lisbon (1958) and Stockholm (1967), and amended in 1979 (Paris Union)

Status on April 15, 2006

State	Date on which State became party to the Convention	Latest Act[1] of the Convention to which State is party and date on which State became party to that Act	
Albania	October 4, 1995	Stockholm	October 4, 1995
Algeria	March 1, 1966	Stockholm	April 20, 1975[2]
Andorra	June 2, 2004	Stockholm	June 2, 2004
Antigua and Barbuda	March 17, 2000	Stockholm	March 17, 2000
Argentina	February 10, 1967	Lisbon	February 10, 1967
		Stockholm	Articles 13 to 30: October 8, 1980
Armenia	December 25, 1991	Stockholm	December 25, 1991[2]
Australia	October 10, 1925	Stockholm	Articles 1 to 12: September 27, 1975
		Stockholm	Articles 13 to 30: August 25, 1972
Austria	January 1, 1909	Stockholm	August 18, 1973
Azerbaijan	December 25, 1995	Stockholm	December 25, 1995
Bahamas	July 10, 1973	Lisbon	July 10, 1973
		Stockholm	Articles 13 to 30: March 10, 1977
Bahrain	October 29, 1997	Stockholm	October 29, 1997
Bangladesh	March 3, 1991	Stockholm	March 3, 1991[2]
Barbados	March 12, 1985	Stockholm	March 12, 1985
Belarus	December 25, 1991	Stockholm	December 25, 1991[2]
Belgium	July 7, 1884	Stockholm	February 12, 1975
Belize	June 17, 2000	Stockholm	June 17, 2000
Benin	January 10, 1967	Stockholm	March 12, 1975
Bhutan	August 4, 2000	Stockholm	August 4, 2000

State	Date on which State became party to the Convention	Latest Act[1] of the Convention to which State is party and date on which State became party to that Act	
Bolivia	November 4, 1993	Stockholm	November 4, 1993
Bosnia and Herzegovina	March 1, 1992	Stockholm	March 1, 1992
Botswana	April 15, 1998	Stockholm	April 15, 1998
Brazil	July 7, 1884	Stockholm	Articles 1 to 12: November 24, 1992
		Stockholm	Articles 13 to 30: March 24, 1975[2]
Bulgaria	June 13, 1921	Stockholm	Articles 1 to 12: May 19 or 27, 1970[3]
		Stockholm	Articles 13 to 30: May 27, 1970
Burkina Faso	November 19, 1963	Stockholm	September 2, 1975
Burundi	September 3, 1977	Stockholm	September 3, 1977
Cambodia	September 22, 1998	Stockholm	September 22, 1998
Cameroon	May 10, 1964	Stockholm	April 20, 1975
Canada	June 12, 1925	Stockholm	Articles 1 to 12: May 26, 1996
		Stockholm	Articles 13 to 30: July 7, 1970
Central African Republic	November 19, 1963	Stockholm	September 5, 1978
Chad	November 19, 1963	Stockholm:	September 26, 1970
Chile	June 14, 1991	Stockholm	June 14, 1991
China[4]	March 19, 1985	Stockholm	March 19, 1985[2]
Colombia	September 3, 1996	Stockholm	September 3, 1996
Comoros	April 3, 2005	Stockholm	April 3, 2005
Congo	September 2, 1963	Stockholm	December 5, 1975
Costa Rica	October 31, 1995	Stockholm	October 31, 1995
Côte d'Ivoire	October 23, 1963	Stockholm	May 4, 1974
Croatia	October 8, 1991	Stockholm	October 8, 1991
Cuba	November 17, 1904	Stockholm	April 8, 1975[2]
Cyprus	January 17, 1966	Stockholm	April 3, 1984
Czech Republic	January 1, 1993	Stockholm	January 1, 1993

State	Date on which State became party to the Convention	Latest Act[1] of the Convention to which State is party and date on which State became party to that Act	
Democratic People's			
Republic of Korea	June 10, 1980	Stockholm	June 10, 1980
Democratic Republic of the Congo	January 31, 1975	Stockholm	January 31, 1975
Denmark[5]............	October 1, 1894	Stockholm	Articles 1 to 12: April 26 or May 19, 1970[3]
		Stockholm	Articles 13 to 30: April 26, 1970
Djibouti	May 13, 2002	Stockholm	May 13, 2002
Dominica	August 7, 1999	Stockholm	August 7, 1999
Dominican Republic	July 11, 1890	The Hague	April 6, 1951
Ecuador	June 22, 1999	Stockholm	June 22, 1999[2]
Egypt	July 1, 1951	Stockholm	March 6, 1975[2]
El Salvador	February 19, 1994	Stockholm	February 19, 1994
Equatorial Guinea	June 26, 1997	Stockholm	June 26, 1997
Estonia	August 24, 1994[6]	Stockholm	August 24, 1994
Finland	September 20, 1921	Stockholm	Articles 1 to 12: October 21, 1975
		Stockholm	Articles 13 to 30: September 15, 1970
France[7]	July 7, 1884	Stockholm	August 12, 1975
Gabon	February 29, 1964	Stockholm	June 10, 1975
Gambia	January 21, 1992	Stockholm	January 21, 1992
Georgia	December 25, 1991	Stockholm	December 25, 1991[2]
Germa	May 1, 1903	Stockholm	September 19, 1970
Ghana	September 28, 1976	Stockholm	September 28, 1976
Greece	October 2, 1924	Stockholm	July 15, 1976
Grenada	September 22, 1998	Stockholm	September 22, 1998
Guatemala	August 18, 1998	Stockholm	August 18, 1998[2]
Guinea	February 5, 1982	Stockholm	February 5, 1982
Guinea-Bissau	June 28, 1988	Stockholm	June 28, 1988

State	Date on which State became party to the Convention	Latest Act[1] of the Convention to which State is party and date on which State became party to that Act	
Guyana	October 25, 1994	Stockholm	October 25, 1994
Haiti	July 1, 1958	Stockholm	November 3, 1983
Holy See	September 29, 1960	Stockholm	April 24, 1975
Honduras	February 4, 1994	Stockholm	February 4, 1994
Hungary	January 1, 1909	Stockholm	Articles 1 to 12: April 26 or May 19, 1970[3]
		Stockholm	Articles 13 to 30: April 26, 1970[2]
Iceland	May 5, 1962	Stockholm	Articles 1 to 12: April 9, 1995
		Stockholm	Articles 13 to 30: December 28, 1984
India	December 7, 1998	Stockholm	December 7, 1998[2]
Indonesia	December 24, 1950	Stockholm	Articles 1 to 12: September 5, 1997
		Stockholm	Articles 13 to 30: December 20, 1979[2]
Iran (Islamic Republic of)	December 16, 1959	Stockholm	March 12, 1999[2]
Iraq	January 24, 1976	Stockholm	January 24, 1976[2]
Ireland	December 4, 1925	Stockholm	Articles 1 to 12: April 26 or May 19, 1970[3]
		Stockholm	Articles 13 to 30: April 26, 1970
Israel	March 24, 1950	Stockholm	Articles 1 to 12: April 26 or May 19, 1970[3]
		Stockholm	Articles 13 to 30: April 26, 1970
Italy	July 7, 1884	Stockholm	April 24, 1977
Jamaica	December 24, 1999	Stockholm	December 24, 1999
Japan	July 15, 1899	Stockholm	Articles 1 to 12: October 1, 1975
		Stockholm	Articles 13 to 30: April 24, 1975
Jordan	July 17, 1972	Stockholm	July 17, 1972
Kazakhstan	December 25, 1991	Stockholm	December 25, 1991[2]

State	Date on which State became party to the Convention	Latest Act[1] of the Convention to which State is party and date on which State became party to that Act	
Kenya	June 14, 1965	Stockholm	October 26, 1971
Kyrgyzstan	December 25, 1991	Stockholm	December 25, 1991[2]
Lao People's Democratic Republic	October 8, 1998	Stockholm	October 8, 1998[2]
Latvia	September 7, 1993[8]	Stockholm	September 7, 1993
Lebanon	September 1, 1924	London	September 30, 1947
		Stockholm	Articles 13 to 30: December 30, 1986[2]
Lesotho	September 28, 1989	Stockholm	September 28, 1989[2]
Liberia	August 27, 1994	Stockholm	August 27, 1994
Libyan Arab Jamahiriya	September 28, 1976	Stockholm	September 28, 1976[2]
Liechtenstein	July 14, 1933	Stockholm	May 25, 1972
Lithuania	May 22, 1994	Stockholm	May 22, 1994
Luxembourg	June 30, 1922	Stockholm	March 24, 1975
Madagascar	December 21, 1963	Stockholm	April 10, 1972
Malawi	July 6, 1964	Stockholm	June 25, 1970
Malaysia	January 1, 1989	Stockholm	January 1, 1989
Mali	March 1, 1983	Stockholm	March 1, 1983
Malta	October 20, 1967	Lisbon	October 20, 1967
		Stockholm	Articles 13 to 30: December 12, 1977[2]
Mauritania	April 11, 1965	Stockholm	September 21, 1976
Mauritius	September 24, 1976	Stockholm	September 24, 1976
Mexico	September 7, 1903	Stockholm	July 26, 1976
Monaco	April 29, 1956	Stockholm	October 4, 1975
Mongolia	April 21, 1985	Stockholm	April 21, 1985[2]
Morocco	July 30, 1917	Stockholm	August 6, 1971
Mozambique	July 9, 1998	Stockholm	July 9, 1998
Namibia	January 1, 2004	Stockholm	January 1, 2004
Nepal	June 22, 2001	Stockholm	June 22, 2001

State	Date on which State became party to the Convention	Latest Act[1] of the Convention to which State is party and date on which State became party to that Act	
Netherlands[9]	July 7, 1884	Stockholm	January 10, 1975
New Zealand[10]	July 29, 1931	London	July 14, 1946
		Stockholm	Articles 13 to 30: June 20, 1984
Nicaragua	July 3, 1996	Stockholm	July 3, 1996[2]
Niger	July 5, 1964	Stockholm	March 6, 1975
Nigeria	September 2, 1963	Lisbon	September 2, 1963
Norway	July 1, 1885	Stockholm	June 13, 1974
Oman	July 14, 1999	Stockholm	July 14, 1999[2]
Pakistan	July 22, 2004	Stockholm	July 22, 2004[2]
Panama	October 19, 1996	Stockholm	October 19, 1996
Papua New Guinea	June 15, 1999	Stockholm	June 15, 1999
Paraguay	May 28, 1994	Stockholm	May 28, 1994
Peru	April 11, 1995	Stockholm	April 11, 1995
Philippines	September 27, 1965	Lisbon	September 27, 1965
		Stockholm	Articles 13 to 30: July 16, 1980
Poland	November 10, 1919	Stockholm	March 24, 1975
Portugal	July 7, 1884	Stockholm	April 30, 1975
Qatar	July 5, 2000	Stockholm	July 5, 2000
Republic of Korea	May 4, 1980	Stockholm	May 4, 1980
Republic of Moldova	December 25, 1991	Stockholm	December 25, 1991[2]
Romania	October 6, 1920	Stockholm	Articles 1 to 12: April 26 or May 19, 1970[3]
		Stockholm	Articles 13 to 30: April 26, 1970[2]
Russian Federation	July 1, 1965[11]	Stockholm	Articles 1 to 12: April 26 or May 19, 1970[3,11]
		Stockholm	Articles 13 to 30: April 26, 1970[2,11]
Rwanda	March 1, 1984	Stockholm	March 1, 1984
Saint Kitts and Nevis	April 9, 1995	Stockholm	April 9, 1995

State	Date on which State became party to the Convention	Latest Act[1] of the Convention to which State is party and date on which State became party to that Act	
Saint Lucia	June 9, 1995	Stockholm	June 9, 1995[2]
Saint Vincent and			
the Grenadines	August 29, 1995	Stockholm	August 29, 1995
San Marino	March 4, 1960	Stockholm	June 26, 1991
Sao Tome and Principe	May 12, 1998	Stockholm	May 12, 1998
Saudi Arabia	March 11, 2004	Stockholm	March 11, 2004
Senegal	December 21, 1963	Stockholm	Articles 1 to 12: April 26 or May 19, 1970[3]
		Stockholm	Articles 13 to 30: April 26, 1970
Serbia and Montenegro	April 27, 1992	Stockholm	April 27, 1992
Seychelles	November 7, 2002	Stockholm	November 7, 2002
Sierra Leone	June 17, 1997	Stockholm	June 17, 1997
Singapore	February 23, 1995	Stockholm	February 23, 1995
Slovakia	January 1, 1993	Stockholm	January 1, 1993
Slovenia	June 25, 1991	Stockholm	June 25, 1991
South Africa	December 1, 1947	Stockholm	March 24, 1975[2]
Spain	July 7, 1884	Stockholm	April 14, 1972
Sri Lanka	December 29, 1952	London	December 29, 1952
		Stockholm	Articles 13 to 30: September 23, 1978
Sudan	April 16, 1984	Stockholm	April 16, 1984
Suriname	November 25, 1975	Stockholm	November 25, 1975
Swaziland	May 12, 1991	Stockholm	May 12, 1991
Sweden	July 1, 1885	Stockholm	Articles 1 to 12: October 9, 1970
Sudan	April 16, 1984	Stockholm	April 16, 1984
Suriname	November 25, 1975	Stockholm	November 25, 1975
Swaziland	May 12, 1991	Stockholm	May 12, 1991
Sweden	July 1, 1885	Stockholm	Articles 1 to 12: October 9, 1970

State	Date on which State became party to the Convention	Latest Act[1] of the Convention to which State is party and date on which State became party to that Act	
		Stockholm	Articles 13 to 30: April 26, 1970
Switzerland	July 7, 1884	Stockholm	Articles 1 to 12: April 26 or May 19, 1970[3]
		Stockholm	Articles 13 to 30: April 26, 1970
Syrian Arab Republic	September 1, 1924	Stockholm	December 13, 2002[2]
Tajikistan	December 25, 1991	Stockholm	December 25, 1991[2]
The former Yugoslav Republic of Macedonia	September 8, 1991	Stockholm	September 8, 1991
Togo	September 10, 1967	Stockholm	April 30, 1975
Tonga	June 14, 2001	Stockholm	June 14, 2001
Trinidad and Tobago	August 1, 1964	Stockholm	August 16, 1988
Tunisia	July 7, 1884	Stockholm	April 12, 1976[2]
Turkey	October 10, 1925	Stockholm	Articles 1 to 12: February 1, 1995
		Stockholm	Articles 13 to 30: May 16, 1976
Turkmenista	December 25, 1991	Stockholm	December 25, 1991[2]
Uganda	June 14, 1965	Stockholm	October 20, 1973
Ukraine	December 25, 1991	Stockholm	December 25, 1991[2]
United Arab Emirates	September 19, 1996	Stockholm	September 19, 1996
United Kingdom[12]	July 7, 1884	Stockholm	Articles 1 to 12: April 26 or May 19, 1970[3]
		Stockholm	Articles 13 to 30: April 26, 1970
United Republic of Tanzania	June 16, 1963	Lisbon	June 16, 1963
		Stockholm	Articles 13 to 30: December 30, 1983

State	Date on which State became party to the Convention	Latest Act[1] of the Convention to which State is party and date on which State became party to that Act	
United States of America[13]	May 30, 1887	Stockholm	Articles 1 to 12: August 25, 1973
		Stockholm	Articles 13 to 30: September 5, 1970
Uruguay	March 18, 1967	Stockholm	December 28, 1979
Uzbekistan	December 25, 1991	Stockholm	December 25, 1991[2]
Venezuela	September 12, 1995	Stockholm	September 12, 1995
Vietnam	March 8, 1949	Stockholm	July 2, 1976[2]
Zambia	April 6, 1965	Lisbon	April 6, 1965
		Stockholm	Articles 13 to 30: May 14, 1977
Zimbabwe	April 18, 1980	Stockholm	December 30, 1981
(Total: 169 States)			

[1] "Stockholm" means the Paris Convention for the Protection of Industrial Property as revised at Stockholm on July 14, 1967, (Stockholm Act); "Lisbon" means the Paris Convention as revised at Lisbon on October 31, 1958 (Lisbon Act); "London" means the Paris Convention as revised at London on June 2, 1934 (London Act); "The Hague" means the Paris Convention as revised at The Hague on November 6, 1925 (Hague Act).

[2] With the declaration provided for in Article 28(2) of the Stockholm Act relating to the International Court of Justice.

[3] These are the alternative dates of entry into force which the Director General of WIPO communicated to the States concerned

[4] The Stockholm Act applies also to the Hong Kong Special Administrative Region with effect from July 1, 1997, and to the Macau Special Administrative Region with effect from December 20, 1999.

[5] Denmark extended the application of the Stockholm Act to the Faroe Islands with effect from August 6, 1971.

[6] Estonia acceded to the Paris Convention (Washington Act, 1911) with effect from February 12, 1924. It lost its independence on August 6, 1940, and regained it on August 20, 1991.

[7] Including all Overseas Departments and Territories.

[8] Latvia acceded to the Paris Convention (Washington Act, 1911) with effect from August 20, 1925. It lost its independence on July 21, 1940, and regained it on August 21, 1991.

[9] Ratification for the Kingdom in Europe, the Netherlands Antilles and Aruba.

[10] The accession of New Zealand to the Stockholm Act, with the exception of Articles 1 to 12, extends to the Cook Islands, Niue and Tokelau.

[11] Date of adherence of the Soviet Union, continued by the Russian Federation as from December 25, 1991.

[12] The United Kingdom extended the application of the Stockholm Act to the Isle of Man with effect from October 29, 1983.

[13] The United States of America extended the application of the Stockholm Act to all territories and possessions of the United States of America, including the Commonwealth of Puerto Rico, as from August 25, 1973.

APPENDIX IV: MEMBER NATIONS OF THE PATENT COOPERATION TREATY (PCT)

Member countries of the PCT as listed in the PCT Applicant's Guide - Volume I - Annex A, dated 20 June 2006.

Name of State followed by Country Code	Date on which State became bound by the PCT*
Albania AL	4 October 1995
Algeria DZ [1]	8 March 2000
Antigua and Barbuda AG	17 March 2000
Armenia AM [1]	25 December 1991
Australia AU	31 March 1980
Austria AT	23 April 1979
Azerbaijan AZ	25 December 1995
Barbados BB	12 March 1985
Belarus BY [1]	25 December 1991
Belgium BE	14 December 1981
Belize BZ	17 June 2000
Benin BJ	26 February 1987
Bosnia and Herzegovina BA	7 September 1996
Botswana BW	30 October 2003
Brazil BR	9 April 1978
Bulgaria BG	21 May 1984
Burkina Faso BF	21 March 1989
Cameroon CM	24 January 1978
Canada CA	2 January 1990
Central African Republic CF	24 January 1978
Chad td	24 January 1978
China CN	1 January 1994
Colombia CO	28 February 2001
Comoros KM	3 April 2005
Congo CG	24 January 1978
Costa Rica CR	3 August 1999
Côte d'Ivoire CI	30 April 1991
Croatia HR	1 July 1998
Cuba CU [1]	16 July 1996

Cyprus CY	1 April 1998
Czech Republic CZ	1 January 1993
Democratic People's Republic of Korea KP	8 July 1980
Denmark DK	1 December 1978
Dominica DM	7 August 1999
Ecuador EC	7 May 2001
Egypt EG	6 September 2003
El Salvador SV	(will become bound on 17 August 2006)
Equatorial Guinea GQ	17 July 2001
Estonia EE	24 August 1994
Finland FI [2]	1 October 1980
France FR [1,3]	25 February 1978
Gabon GA	24 January 1978
Gambia GM	9 December 1997
Georgia GE [1]	25 December 1991
Germany DE	24 January 1978
Ghana GH	26 February 1997
Greece GR	9 October 1990
Grenada GD	22 September 1998
Guinea GN	27 May 1991
Guinea-Bissau GW	12 December 1997
Honduras HN	20 June 2006
Hungary HU [1]	27 June 1980
Iceland IS	23 March 1995
India IN [1]	7 December 1998
Indonesia ID [1]	5 September 1997
Ireland IE	1 August 1992
Israel IL	1 June 1996
Italy IT	28 March 1985
Japan JP	1 October 1978
Kazakhstan KZ [1]	25 December 1991
Kenya KE	8 June 1994
Kyrgyzstan KG [1]	25 December 1991

Lao People's Democratic Republic LA	14 June 2006
Latvia LV	7 September 1993
Lesotho LS	21 October 1995
Liberia LR	27 August 1994
Libyan Arab Jamahiriya LY	15 September 2005
Liechtenstein LI	19 March 1980
Lithuania LT	5 July 1994
Luxembourg LU	30 April 1978
Madagascar MG	24 January 1978
Malawi MW	24 January 1978
Malaysia MY[1]	(will become bound on 16 August 2006)
Mali ML	19 October 1984
Mauritania MR	13 April 1983
Mexico MX	1 January 1995
Monaco MC	22 June 1979
Mongolia MN	27 May 1991
Morocco MA	8 October 1999
Mozambique MZ [1]	18 May 2000
Namibia NA	1 January 2004
Netherlands NL [4]	10 July 1979
New Zealand NZ	1 December 1992
Nicaragua NA	6 March 2003
Niger NE	21 March 1993
Nigeria NG	8 May 2005
Norway NO [2]	1 January 1980
Oman OM [1]	26 October 2001
Papua New Guinea PG	14 June 2003
Philippines PH	17 August 2001
Poland PL [2]	25 December 1990
Portugal PT	24 November 1992
Republic of Korea KR	10 August 1984
Republic of Moldova MD [1]	25 December 1991
Romania RO [1]	23 July 1979

Russian Federation RU [1]	29 March 1978
Saint Kitts and Nevis KN	27 October 2005
Saint Lucia LC [1]	30 August 1996
Saint Vincent and the Grenadines VC [1]	6 August 2002
San Marino SM	14 December 2004
Senegal SN	24 January 1978
Serbia and Montenegro YU	1 February 1997
Seychelles SC	7 November 2002
Sierra Leone SL	17 June 1997
Singapore SG	23 February 1995
Slovakia SK	1 January 1993
Slovenia SI	1 March 1994
South Africa ZA [1]	16 March 1999
Spain ES	16 November 1989
Sri Lanka LK	26 February 1982
Sudan SD	16 April 1984
Swaziland SZ	20 September 1994
Sweden SE [2]	17 May 1978
Switzerland CH	24 January 1978
Syrian Arab Republic SY	26 June 2003
Tajikistan TJ [1]	25 December 1991
The former Yugoslav Republic of Macedonia MK	10 August 1995
Togo TG	24 January 1978
Trinidad and Tobago TT	10 March 1994
Tunisia TN [1]	10 December 2001
Turkey TR	1 January 1996
Turkmenistan TM [1]	25 December 1991
Uganda UG	9 February 1995
Ukraine UA [1]	25 December 1991
United Arab Emirates AE	10 March 1999
United Kingdon GB [5]	24 January 1978
United Republic of Tanzania TZ	14 September 1999
United States of America US [6, 7]	24 January 1978

Uzebekistan UZ [1]	25 December 1991
Viet Nam VN	10 March 1993
Zambia	15 November 2001
Zimbabwe ZW	11 June 1997

* All PCT Contracting States are bound by Chapter II of the PCT relating to the international preliminary examination.
1. With the declaration provided for in Article 64(5)
2. With the declaration provided for in Article 64(2)(a)(ii)
3. Including all Overseas Departments and Territories.
4. Ratification for the Kingdom in Europe, the Netherlands Antilles and Aruba.
5. Extends to the Isle of Man.
6. With the declarations provided for in Articles 64(3)(a) and 64(4)(a).
7. Extends to all areas for which the United States of America has international responsibility.

APPENDIX V: CROSS REFERENCE OF TREATY MEMBERSHIPS

Countries and jurisdictions that share membership in treaties with the U.S.

PC - the Paris Convention	PCT - the Patent Cooperation Treaty
EP – the European Patent Convention	PT – Priority Treaty

Country or Jurisdiction	PC	PCT	EP	PT
Albania	x	x		
Algeria	x	x		
Andorra	x			
Antigua and Barbuda	x	x		
Argentina	x			
Armenia	x	x		
Australia	x	x		
Austria	x	x	x	
Azerbaijan	x	x		
Bahamas	x			
Bahrain	x			
Bangladesh	x			
Barbados	x	x		
Belarus	x	x		
Belgium	x	x	x	
Belize	x	x		
Benin	x	x		
Bhutan	x			
Bolivia	x			
Bosnia and Herzegovina	x	x		
Botswana	x	x		

Brazil	X	X		
Bulgaria	X	X	X	
Burkina Faso	X	X		
Burundi	X			
Cambodia	X			
Cameroon	X	X		
Canada	X	X		
Central African Republic	X	X		
Chad	X	X		
Chile	X			
China	X	X		X
Colombia	X	X		
Comoros	X	X		
Congo	X	X		
Costa Rica	X	X		X
Côte d'Ivoire	X	X		
Croatia	X	X		
Cuba	X	X		
Cyprus	X	X	X	
Czech Republic	X	X	X	
Democratic People's	X	X		
Democratic Republic of the Congo	X			
Denmark	X	X	X	
Djibouti	X			
Dominica	X	X		
Dominican Republic	X			
Ecuador	X	X		

Egypt	x	x		
El Salvador	x	x		
Equatorial Guinea	x	x		
Estonia	x	x	x	
Finland	x	x	x	
France	x	x	x	
Gabon	x	x		
Gambia	x	x		
Georgia	x	x		
Germany	x	x	x	
Ghana	x	x		
Greece	x	x		
Grenada	x	x		
Guatemala	x			
Guinea	x	x		
Guinea-Bissau	x	x		
Guyana	x			
Haiti	x			
Hellenic Republic			x	
Holy See	x			
Honduras	x			
Hungary	x	x	x	
Iceland	x	x	x	
India	x	x		x
Indonesia	x	x		
Iran (Islamic Republic of)	x			
Iraq	x			
Ireland	x		x	

Israel	x			
Italy	x	x	x	
Jamaica	x			
Japan	x	x		
Jordan	x			
Kazakhstan	x	x		
Kenya	x	x		
Kyrgyzstan	x	x		
Lao People's Democratic Republic	x	x		
Latvia	x	x	x	
Lebanon	x			
Lesotho	x	x		
Liberia	x	x		
Libyan Arab Jamahiriya	x	x		
Liechtenstein	x	x	x	
Lithuania	x	x	x	
Luxembourg	x	x	x	
Madagascar	x	x		
Malawi	x	x		
Malaysia	x	x		
Mali	x	x		
Malta	x			
Mauritania	x	x		
Mauritius	x			
Mexico	x	x		
Monaco	x	x	x	
Mongolia	x	x		
Morocco	x	x		

Mozambique	x	x		
Namibia	x	x		
Nepal	x			
Netherlands	x	x	x	
New Zealand	x	x		
Nicaragua	x	x		
Niger	x	x		
Nigeria	x	x		
Norway	x	x		
Oman	x	x		
Pakistan	x			
Panama	x			
Papua New Guinea	x	x		
Paraguay	x			
Peru	x			
Philippines	x	x		
Poland	x	x	x	
Portugal	x	x	x	
Qatar	x			
Republic of Korea	x			
Republic of Korea	x	x		
Republic of Moldova	x	x		
Romania	x	x	x	
Russian Federation	x	x		
Rwanda	x			
Saint Kitts and Nevis	x	x		
Saint Lucia	x	x		

Saint Vincent and the Grenadines	x	x		
San Marino	x	x		
Sao Tome and Principe	x			
Saudi Arabia	x			
Senegal	x	x		
Serbia and Montenegro	x	x		
Seychelles	x	x		
Sierra Leone	x	x		
Singapore	x	x		
Slovakia	x	x	x	
Slovenia	x	x	x	
South Africa	x	x		
Spain	x	x	x	
Sri Lanka	x	x		
Sudan	x	x		
Suriname	x			
Swaziland	x	x		
Sweden	x	x	x	
Switzerland	x	x	x	
Syrian Arab Republic	x	x		
Tajikistan	x	x		
The former Yugoslav Republic of Macedonia	x	x		
Thailand				x
Togo	x	x		
Tonga	x			
Trinidad and Tobago	x	x		
Tunisia	x	x		
Turkey	x	x	x	

Turkmenistan	x	x		
Uganda	x	x		
Ukraine	x	x		
United Arab Emirates	x	x		
United Kingdom	x	x	x	
United Republic of Tanzania	x	x		
United States of America	x	x		
Uruguay	x			
Uzbekistan	x	x		
Venezuela	x			
Viet Nam	x	x		
Zambia	x	x		
Zimbabwe	x	x		

Glossary

Abandonment - An application that has been declared abandoned is no longer pending. The most common reason for abandonment occurs when the USPTO does not receive a response to an Office Action letter from an applicant within six months from the date the Office action letter was mailed. Abandoned applications can be revived or reinstated in certain circumstances.

Abstract - a brief summary of a patent, usually printed on the first page of the application.

Agent (patent) - One who is not an attorney but is authorized to represent the applicant(s) before the Patent Office; that is, an individual who is registered to practice before the Office.

Anticipation - Occurs when the prior art indicates that a patent application lacks novelty.

Apparatus claim - a claim which describes a device or product.

Applicant - the person filing the patent application. In the U.S., patent applications are always filed in the name of the inventors, who may then assign their rights to, for example, their employer. In foreign countries, the assignee and the applicant are the same.

Application - A document seeking patent protection and filed with the U.S. Patent and Trademark Office or a patent office outside of the United States. In the United States, the application must include a description of the invention that would enable a person of ordinary skill in the art to make and use it; at least one claim; drawings; and purpose of the invention.

Apportionment of Profit - A measure of damages in patent-infringement litigation; refers to dividing profits upon the sale of a particular product according to the percentage of cost or sale price. When the entire product is patented or the patented component contributes essentially all of the market value, apportionment of profit is not required.

Assignee - The person(s) or company to whom all or limited rights under a patent are legally transferred.

Assignment - Selling a patent or application and the document of sale. Also a transfer of ownership of a trademark application or registration from one person or company to another. Recording assignments with the Patent Office Assignment Services Division is recommended to maintain clear title to pending trademark applications and registrations.

Best Mode - A patent applicant is required to disclose the best means known to him or her of practicing the invention as of the date the application is filed.

Claim - That part of the patent which defines the limits of the grant of rights. Claims are composed using obsolete legal terms. Every claim starts with an upper case letter — only one is permitted — and ends with a period — again, only one is permitted — and each name in the claim must be defined before it is used. The claims become the actual monopoly that is given when the patent is granted.

Co-inventor - One of the people who contributed to the idea of an invention. Merely contributing to reduction to practice does not make one a co-inventor.

Conception - The idea of an invention, followed by reduction to practice to complete the act of invention.

Critical Date - The date of placing on sale, publication, or public or commercial use of an invention. Statute prevents a U.S. patent application from being filed after one year.

Counterpart - An application filed by one applicant in a foreign patent office that is substantially similar to the patent application filed with the USPTO.

Crowded Art - This refers to an area of technology in which there have been a large number of inventions.

Dependent claim - A claim that refers to and further limits a preceding claim. A dependent claim includes every limitation of the claim from which it depends. Claims that do not depend from another are referred to as independent claims.

Deposit account - An account established in the USPTO for the convenience of paying any fees due, in ordering services offered by the USPTO or copies of records, for example.

Design patent - May be granted to anyone who invents a new design for an article; covers the ornamental appearance of a useful object.

Detail view - A part of another figure, enlarged, referred to usually by dotted or dashed lines.

Disclosure document - A document disclosing an invention signed by the inventor that is forwarded to the USPTO only as evidence of the date of conception of the invention.

Divisional - The rule is: one invention to a patent and one patent to an invention. If the examiner believes that two embodiments were two independently patentable inventions, they may be split into two applications for two patents. The second is called a "divisional."

Doctrine of Equivalents -A rule that an element in a claim also includes equivalent structures if they do the same thing in the same manner to reach the same result. The doctrine is used if an accused device does not literally infringe a claim because an element of the claim is different from the device, but the patentee believes that the element used in the device is the same as the one in the claim. Under the judicially created doctrine of equivalents, one may be held liable as an infringer even if one does not literally infringe a patent. It is an equitable concept employed to prevent someone from getting the benefit of the invention by making a minor change that avoids literal infringement.

Double Patenting - An inventive entity cannot obtain claims for two patents for the same invention even if one is a variation of an invention.

Embodiments - Variations of an invention; or a manner in which an invention can be made, used, practiced, or expressed.

Enforceability of patent - The right of a patent owner to sue for infringement against a person or company that makes, uses, or sells the claimed invention without permission. A patent's period of enforceability of is the term of the patent plus six years.

eTEAS – The Electronic Trademark Examination Application allows the public to complete various trademark filings and transactions online.

European Patent Convention (EPC) – Made up of 20 western European countries as of November 2000. A patent application filed under this convention will be effective in each of the countries designated by the applicant.

Examination - The review of a patent application by an examiner.

Examining attorney - A USPTO employee who examines an application for registration of a registered trademark to see

whether it meets legal and regulatory requirements.

Experimental Use - There are a number of statutes that bar filing for a U.S. patent application more than one year after initially placing on sale, publication, or public use of an invention. If the use was experimental it is not counted in computing the one-year period.

Express mail mailing label - Patent correspondence delivered to the USPTO via the "Express Mail Post Office to Addressee" service of the United States Postal Service, considered filed in the Patent Office on the date of deposit with the USPS, shown on the mailing label. The filing date for Trademark documents is not the same as for patent documents.

Fanciful marks - Terms that have been invented to function as a trademark. Such marks may be words that are unknown in the language (Coca-Cola, Xerox).

Final Data Capture (FDC) - After all requirements have been met for issuance of a patent, the application is forwarded to the Final Data Capture (FDC) stage of the process. An Issue Notification is the next step and is mailed about three weeks before the issue date of the patent.

File wrapper - The folder collection of documents maintained by the USPTO, containing a complete official record of proceedings from the filing of the initial patent application to the issued patent.

Final office action (rejection) - An Office action on the second or any subsequent examination or consideration that closes a non-provisional patent application.

First to File - With European patents, the patent is awarded to the first person to file an application rather than who was the first to invent. This is the present law in all countries other than the USA and the Philippines.

GATT - General Agreement on Tariffs and Trade signed by President Clinton on December 8, 1994, extending patents filed on or after June 8, 1995 to 20 years from the filing date rather than 17 years from the date the patent was granted.

Gist of the Invention - The "heart of the invention," referring to the unique features of the invention.

Hypothetical Person Skilled in the Art - Standard applied to determine whether the invention would have been obvious at the time the invention was made to one having ordinary skill in the art.

Inventors Assistance Center (IAC) - call 1-800-786-9199 or 703-308-4357

Improvement Patent - A patent issued on an application filed later in time than a prior application. It builds on a previously disclosed invention.

Identification of goods and services - Statement of the goods and services included in that must appear in an application for a patent.

Indefiniteness of Claim - Claims must be definite enough to provide a standard for a third party to determine if another invention would be an infringement of the claims.

Infringement - Occurs when someone makes, uses, sells, places on sale, or imports into the United States a claimed invention. A company or person who owns the patent has the right to stop an infringer from making, using, or selling an infringing device or method. See Literal Infringement.

Intellectual property - Creations of the mind that can be protected by patents, trademarks, copyrights, or trade secrets.

Interference - Under U.S. law, a patent goes to the first person to invent an invention, as opposed to "first to file" systems in most other countries, where the first person to file an application gets the patent. A priority proceeding in the U.S. Patent and Trademark Office in which two or more parties present evidence of conception and reduction to practice with a view toward proving who first invented the invention.

International Preliminary Examining Authority (IPEA) - A national office or an intergovernmental organization to examine reports on inventions that are the subject of international applications.

Invention - A patentable invention in the United States is one that is useful, novel, and un-obvious to one skilled in the art at the time the invention was made. It consists of two steps: conception and reduction to practice.

Issue date - The date that a patent application becomes a U.S. patent, that is, enforceable. All U.S. patents are issued on Tuesdays.

Jeppson Claim (Also Jepson Claim) - A special claim form which starts "An improved ___ _____ (name of invention) of the kind having..." followed by the prior art elements of the claim. The form then reads "in which the improvement comprises," followed by the novel part of the invention. Jeppson claims are similar to the "two part claim form" required in the European Patent Office and some other foreign patent systems.

Joint application - An application in which the invention is presented as belonging to more than one person.

License - A transfer of patent rights that does not amount to an assignment. A license does not give the licensee legal title to a patent.

Literal Infringement - A

product, process, apparatus, or composition of matter that meets every recital of a claim (literally).

Legal Instruments Examiner (LIE) - A position classification for administrative USPTO employees charged with docketing cases and providing other support for the workflow and examination of applications.

Likelihood of confusion - If a conflict exists between your mark and a registered mark, the examining attorney will refuse registration on the ground of likelihood of confusion. It may be enough that the marks are similar and the goods and services related. If a conflict exists between an unregistered mark and a registered mark, the examining attorney will refuse registration on the ground of likelihood of confusion.

Long-Felt Need - A problem facing a particular technical area that has gone unsolved for a prolonged period. The presumption is if the solution had been obvious to those skilled in the art, they would have solved the problem.

Lost Profits - A measure of damages keyed to the profits that could have been the patentee's, but were lost to the infringer.

Maintenance Fees - In the United States, maintenance fees or taxes must be paid at 3.5, 7.5, and 11.5 years after the date of issue of a US patent to maintain the patent in force. If the maintenance fees are not paid, the patent expires at the end of the surcharge period (4.5, 8.5, or 12.5 years after issue).

"Means plus function" - A way of describing an invention in a claim by what it does, rather than what it is. Court cases have limited the scope of "means plus function" language to mean only the "means" shown and described in the description.

Markush Doctrine - A way of listing a group of claimed materials. An inventor writes, "selected from the group consisting of A, B, and C." The alternative to claiming it this way would be to write numerous claims saying, "In the invention in claim 1, group A is chlorine," and then drafting additional claims for each possible group. While this type of claim is commonly used in chemical patents, it can also be used in mechanical patents.

Multiple dependent claim - A claim which depends on more than one preceding claim either directly or indirectly.

Non-final office action - An Office action made by the examiner where the applicant is entitled to reply and request reconsideration or further examination, with or without making an amendment; an office action letter that raises new issues and usually is the first phase of the examination process.

Notice - Placing the word "patent" with the patent number on articles made by the patentee. If the patentee fails to mark his or her products, he or she may not recover damages for infringement.

Notice of abandonment - A notification from the Patent Office that an application has been declared to be abandoned and is no longer pending. The applicant has a deadline of two months from the issue date of the notice to file a petition to revive the application or a request to reinstate the application.

Notice of allowance (NOA) - A notification to an applicant of entitlement to a patent under the law and requesting payment of a specified issue fee within three months; notice that a specific mark has survived the opposition period following publication in the Official Gazette and has consequently been allowed for registration. Receiving a notice of allowance is another step on the way to registration; it does not mean that the mark has registered but is another step toward registration.

Notice of Appeal - An applicant's document to initiate an appeal of an examiner's rejection to the Board of Patent Appeals and Interferences.

Notice of publication - A written statement from the USPTO notifying an applicant that its mark will be published in the Official Gazette. Any party who believes it may be damaged by registration has 30 days to file an opposition to registration.

Novelty - One of the conditions that an invention must meet to be patentable. Novelty is defined as being not patented, or described in a publication, or in public use, or on sale by others before you invented it, or by anyone (including you) more than a year before you applied for a patent.

Obviousness - If the invention could readily be deduced at the time the invention was made from publicly available information (prior art) by a person of ordinary skill in that art, it is obvious.

Office Action - An official written communication from an examiner in the USPTO. More than 85 percent of applications are rejected.

On Sale - If an inventor places an invention on sale more than a year before a U.S. patent application is filed, he or she is not eligible for a valid patent. This is sometimes referred to as the "on-sale bar to a patent."

Opposition - Time period allowed for an interested party to post opposition to granting a patent.

Original filing basis - The basis set forth in the application as initially filed.

Patent Application Locating and Monitoring system (PALM) - An internal USPTO system that is the source of status information.

Parent Application - Applied to an earlier application of the inventor about an invention.

Patent - The grant by the government of the right to stop others from making, using, or selling an invention. Patents that cover structural or functional aspects of products, composition, and processes are utility patents. Others are design patents covering ornamental designs of useful objects and plant patents covering new varieties of living plants.

Patent Agent – A person licensed to prosecute patent applications in the USPTO; a patent agent must have a degree in engineering or one of the "hard" sciences and pass an examination given by the USPTO.

Patent number - Unique number assigned to a patent application when it issues as a patent.

Patent pending - A phrase that

often appears on manufactured items, meaning that someone has applied for a patent on an invention that is contained in the manufactured item. It is a warning that a patent may issue that would cover the item and that copiers may infringe when the patent issues. Using the "patent pending" phrase to an item when no patent application has been made can result in a fine. A provisional application will support a "patent pending" marking.

Plant patent - May be granted to anyone who invents or discovers and asexually reproduces any distinct, new variety of plant.

Preamble: The introductory clause of a patent claim.

Preferred Embodiment - Can usually be interpreted as the best mode known to the inventor of executing the invention.

Priority action - A letter in which an examining attorney sets forth requirements that the applicant must meet before an application can be approved for publication. The benefit of a priority action is that, if the applicant responds within two months, the application will be given priority in processing the response.

Pro Se - Used to designate an independent inventor who files an application without the services of a licensed representative.

Provisional Application - A patent application which reserves a filing date for the material in the application but will never be examined or become a patent. As a result of GATT, an applicant can file a patent specification complying with U.S. disclosure standards and get the filing date as a priority date for a complete patent application filed within one year thereafter claiming the benefit. It has the benefit of the date of filing the full application for purposes of the 20-year patent term.

Provisional rights - The ability to ask for pre-issue damages is called provisional rights.

Read On - If a claim reads on prior art, the claim is invalid. A claim must read on an accused device for infringement to occur.

Reduction to Practice - The physical part of the inventive process that completes the process of invention.

Re-examination proceeding - At any time during the enforceability of a patent anyone may file a request for the USPTO to conduct a second examination of any claim of the patent on the basis of prior art patents which that person posits to be pertinent to the patent and believes to have a bearing on the patentability.

Registration - Federal registration of trademarks has several advantages, including notice to the public of the registrant's claim of ownership of the mark, the exclusive right to use the mark, the ability to bring an action concerning the mark in federal court, and the use of the U.S. registration to obtain registration in foreign countries.

Registration number - A registered patent attorney or agent is assigned a registration number that they must include on patent correspondence and forms when representing others before the USPTO. Individual applicants should leave this field blank on patent forms.

Renewal Application - A sworn document, filed by the owner of a registration, to avoid the expiration of a registration.

Renewal Fees - An applicant must pay the patent office to keep the patent. In the United States, these fees are called maintenance fees.

Research Disclosure - Defensive-type documents published to give companies and inventors "freedom of use" rather than legal protection. Their publication prevents the invention described from being patented.

Revocation - Termination of the protection given to a patent on one or more grounds, such as lack of novelty.

Search - After a trademark application is filed, the USPTO will conduct a search of their records for conflicting marks as part of the official examination process to determine whether the mark applied for can be registered. The USPTO advises applicants or their representatives to search the records before filing the application. A search may be conducted through TESS, or by visiting the Trademark Public Search Library, free to the public in Alexandria, VA. Also, certain information may be searched at a Patent and Trademark Depository Library.

Service mark - A word, name, or symbol that indicates the source of services, distinguishing them from the others' services. A service mark is the same as a trademark except that it identifies the source of a service.

Small Entity - A small entity has fewer than 500 employees or is a non-profit or academic institution. Often the term denotes the smaller, newer, and more entrepreneurial inventor entities, from the older, larger established ones.

Specification - That part of the patent which describes the invention in sufficient detail so that someone knowledgeable in the art could practice it; the main part of the patent.

Statutory disclaimer - The owner of a patent may give up all rights to a claim of the patent.

Suggestive mark - A mark that, when applied to the goods or services, requires the ability

to reach a conclusion about the nature of those goods or services.

TARR Trademark Application and Registration Retrieval system - USPTO's online database for monitoring federal trademark applications and registrations.

TESS Trademark Electronic Search System - USPTO's online database for searching pending, registered, and dead federal trademarks. It is free and intended for use by the general public.

USPTO (Patent and Trademark Office) - Office of the U.S. Department of Commerce responsible for examining and issuing patents.

Valid - Only a court can hold a patent is invalid. Many patents are informally referred to as being invalid to indicate that a court would likely rule them invalid.

Willful Infringement - Conduct that constitutes an illegal use of another's patented invention where the infringer has no reason to believe that its actions are legal.

Index